WHAT GOD MEANT

© 2009 Kabbalah Centre International, Inc.

Kabbalah Publishing is a registered DBA of
Kabbalah Centre International, Inc.

For further information:

The Kabbalah Centre
155 E. 48th St., New York, NY 10017
1062 S. Robertson Blvd., Los Angeles, CA 90035

1.800.Kabbalah www.kabbalah.com

First Edition
July 2009
ISBN13: 978-1-57189-639-1

Design: HL Design (Hyun Min Lee) www.hldesignco.com

WHAT
GOD
MEANT

⇜ Volume 1 ⇝
A Collection of
Teachings on Genesis

MICHAEL BERG

TABLE OF CONTENTS

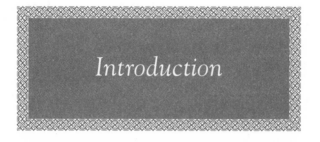

Introduction

This book is a collection of lectures that I have given over the past few years. Every week I have the privilege of instructing Kabbalah Centre teachers all over the world as well as countless students on ukabbalah.com and in the local community wherever I am during that Shabbat. I prepare for my lectures by reading from the texts of many kabbalists with the goal to always find something new, something that inspires me to change, to grow to be closer to the Creator. I read many, many interesting and important commentaries, but there are a special few that excite and inspire me, and it is my hope that these lessons inspire you to grow and change as well.

The kabbalists teach that the Torah, the Bible, is not a historic document, nor is it a static book of teachings and stories; rather it is a powerful source of Light and energy that is intended to manifest differently for every person, for all time. We read one portion a week, and within that portion there are lessons both old and new.

The kabbalists teach us that every week the stories we read and the lessons we learn do not simply just further our understanding. Instead we know that the Light and energy that was revealed when these stories were first occurred becomes awakened again when we read them. When we learn about the revelation at Sinai, for instance, that same Light and energy is reawakened in our world, and we can connect to it and draw on it. The souls of the great spiritual giants we read about come back to our world to support us, teach us, and share their Light through these stories. Therefore, the study of these stories brings much more than inspiration and familiarity with the lessons they contain. Studying these tales actually supplies us with the ability to connect in deep and powerful ways to these amazing souls. It is this assistance that can truly enable us to accomplish our spiritual goals and reveal our potential.

The kabbalists teach that when we study on our own we merit some revelations and understanding, depending on our own spiritual level and work. But when we teach others we are shown and taught even beyond our level for the sake of the students with whom we share. I know without a doubt that the only reason I can find inspiration within these texts is because of my good fortune that there are people willing to listen to me. Certainly whatever good one can find in this book is not due to my studies but rather due to those who are willing to listen. I would like to thank all of the teachers, students, readers, and listeners for allowing wisdom that is beyond me to be revealed.

Almost none of these lessons are my own but are largely culled from the teachings of the great kabbalists over many centuries. In keeping with a tradition of passing on this wisdom that has persisted for thousands of years, I have used the names of their books and works when sharing their teachings.

In preparing this book we struggled with the question of language and form. We initially thought we would change the original conversational tone of these lectures to more formal written prose, but we decided that they could best achieve their purpose by remaining closer to the original form. This does create interesting challenges for you as a reader, but it is my hope that by hewing as close as possible to the original lectures we are allowing you to receive the most benefit.

Although we translated most of the ancient texts and words into English, there are a few words that appear frequently in their original Hebrew form. One such word is *Midrash*. The *Midrash* refers to the Torah commentaries from approximately 2000 years ago, which were revealed at about the same time as the *Zohar*. Many of the spiritual giants that appear in the *Zohar* appear in the *Midrash* as well. The *Midrash* is a fundamental text upon which many of the kabbalists base their commentaries and interpretations.

The other words that appear in their original form are uniquely important. The main purpose of the study of Kabbalah is to bring each of us the personal fulfillment, joy, and peace that we are meant to enjoy. But the long-term goal of the study and dissemination of this wisdom is to bring about a complete change in our world—a total removal of pain, suffering, and death. This end is called the *Gemar haTikkun*, the end of the correction of humanity. In the Bible, this new era is sometimes referred to as *Mashiach* (Messiah), which Kabbalistically is not focused on a single person, but more significantly refers to the change achieved by the work of humanity. In the Bible the promise of reaching this goal is called *bila hamavet lanetzach*, or the end of death forever. We have used these three terms throughout the book. It is my hope that this book can move us all closer to this reality, in fulfillment of the prophecy, "And God will wipe away all the tears from all the faces...," when all pain, suffering and death will be removed from our world.

Blessings and Light,

Michael

Beresheet

THE HOLY COMMUNITY

On the Shabbat morning of Beresheet, I was not feeling very well. I considered whether I should pray at The Kabbalah Centre, or at home. Should I give the lecture or rest?

Then I remembered a very important idea; one of the lessons we will learn from the story of Beresheet. As Beresheet is the first reading of the Torah and thus falls on the first Shabbat of the year, it is important to awaken this lesson within us all.

Why do we come to services together at The Kabbalah Centre? We don't simply come together to make the connections; to listen and receive the Light from the Torah (Bible). We come here because there is an awesome power, a tremendous extra infusion of Light, that happens simply because we are together.

The *Zohar* speaks about the fact that each of the seven days of Creation is called by a number: second day, third day, fourth day, fifth day. But, regarding the first day of Creation, the Torah says is not *yom rishon* (first day), as we might expect, but *yom echad* (one day), a singular day—unity.

The kabbalists explain that when people come together in unity to reveal Light, the Light that they reveal in this way is greater than any Light they reveal in any other way. As I was thinking about this message, I realized that every one of us has our routine—even our spiritual routine—so we have to be very mindful not to allow this weekly activity of coming together to become simply another routine.

Yes, we make our connections, and yes, we listen to the Torah. But even greater than this is the power of our gathering, because it is the act itself of gathering that allows a greater Light to be revealed. That is why I come here. Not because this is our spiritual routine. And not because The Kabbalah Centre is simply a place to make connections, where we listen to and reveal the Light of the Torah. We come together because there is something unique, something magical that occurs when we gather here every Shabbat. It's especially important that we remind ourselves of this on the first Shabbat of the year.

Our individual connections pale in comparison to the Light that we reveal when we participate in Shabbat together. This Shabbat morning, as I was making my decision whether to go to the Centre or stay home, I had a clear vision of this tremendous Light. The *Zohar* says that, unfortunately, we do not truly see. Most of us see the physical, but we do not see the spiritual. If we had the ability to see spiritually, we would see the great Light that is generated when we come together in unity. If we could see this, never again, would there be any doubt in our minds about the need to gather, not simply for our individual connections, meditations, prayers, and Torah but to come together as one to a physical place.

In speaking of Beresheet, the kabbalists say that giving others the ability to do their spiritual work is even more important than doing our own spiritual work. Our thoughts should be twofold: On one hand, yes, I want to make my own connection and reveal Light for myself and my family for this week; but I also want to be a conduit, a tool to allow everyone else here to reveal their Light, to receive their Light on Shabbat. This dual consciousness—of desiring to make our own connection, as well as wanting to be a conduit for others to make their connection—is necessary in order for us to partake of the Light of the *echad* (one); the Light that is created by unity, by participating together.

Now, we understand that the reason we gather together on Shabbat is not only because we reveal much more Light in unity than we could individually, but also because we recognize that if we want to partake of that Light, we are required to put something in. On Shabbat, our consciousness should be that we come together not only to reveal Light for ourselves and for the world, but we gather to help everyone else to reveal their Light. Now our consciousness is in the right place to allow us to partake of the tremendous Light that is revealed through our gathering.

This leads me to an idea that we have spoken about before: the power of "the community"—and the importance of this reawakening during this, the first Shabbat of the year. Every one of us has our own spiritual work, our own physical work, and our own families, but if we want to truly partake of the gift that is this community, we have to be putting in, in great ways or small. Therefore, we have to make sure to ask ourselves: "What am I doing not for my own spiritual connection but to further the growth of the community?"

It is important, certainly in Beresheet, in this "beginning," this first of the Bible readings of the year, that we understand the significance and value of this first reading, as well as make a commitment that throughout the year we will constantly be contributing to the growth and strength of this community. As we said, the amount of Light that we can receive through our own connections is limited, and pales in comparison, to the amount of Light that we can receive collectively on Shabbat—and during the year—by having everyone assist in revealing our Light. That is why it's so important that we make this commitment to give to the community.

This Shabbat morning as I was considering whether to come to the Centre or not, I was reminded that one of the aspects of Beresheet, is that one can spend literally a lifetime studying just this first section of the Torah (Bible). It is deep and inspiring, and fascinating on so many levels. As a rule when I teach, I try to find something that inspires me, something that can push us forward in our spiritual work. However, there is so much we can cover with regard to Beresheet, and I would like to share a few major points with you.

WE NEED THE OPPONENT TO ACHIEVE
OUR ULTIMATE POTENTIAL

One of the significant stories in Beresheet is the tale of Adam and Eve, the snake, and the Tree of Knowledge of Good and Evil. The literal story begins with the Creator putting Adam and Eve in *Gan Eden* (the Garden of Eden). Although we speak of these stories in literal terms, they all, in fact, refer to the spiritual dimensions; none of this was physical in the beginning. When the Creator puts Adam and Eve in the Garden of Eden, He tells them that they may eat from all the trees of the Garden except one, *Etz haDaat Tov veRa* (the Tree of Knowledge of Good and Evil). The snake then approaches Eve and tricks her into eating of the Tree of Knowledge Good and Evil, and when Eve gives some to Adam, they both fall spiritually—and death enters our world.

In writing about Eve, the Ohr haChaim (Rabbi Chaim ben Attar 1696-1743) asks, "How did this happen? How did Eve fall?" I find this question fascinating. The Ohr haChaim tells us: "Eve was not so much at fault here. Eve did not fathom that there could possibly be a creation in our world that was not positive."

One of the most important topics that we learn about in Kabbalah is what we call the "ego," also known as the *Desire to Receive for the Self Alone*, and referred to by some people as Satan, the negative force, or the Opponent. Eve, however, had no awareness of the existence of this negative force. She came into this beautiful world and her understanding was that it was all good: Adam was good, Eve was good, the animals were good, the trees were good. When the Opponent came to her in the form of the snake, she had no idea that he was trying to trick her.

The Ohr haChaim continues, "If Eve had known that there was an Opponent in this world, of course she would have taken time to think through what his words meant and eventually figured out that what he was saying did not make sense. But she had no concept." This awakens within us an appreciation of that most basic of lessons: There is an Opponent and we have to be wary. If Eve had had that one piece of information, we all would not be here. This revelation awakens both a profound understanding of, and an appreciation for, what we learn from this lesson.

The Ohr haChaim asks the question, which is one that many of us have asked as well: "Why was the snake created?" This is something I reminded myself about on this Shabbat morning: The only way that we can remove pain and suffering and death from our world is to overcome the Opponent that is pushing us, that is making us doubt, that is trying to make us fall. The snake gives us the ability to grow—if not for the snake we would all be born into this world "good" and never have the opportunity to achieve the level of *bilha hamavet lanetzach* (removal of pain, suffering, and death from our world). If the purpose of our work in this world were not to achieve this goal of *bilha hamavet lanetzach*, there would be no need for the snake, or for him to be as strong as he is.

There are two types of people in this world. There are good people, those who make some mistakes, but, in general, are kind people. Then there are those who have fallen, who have done damage. Which is better: To be a good person, or to be someone who has fallen? The Ohr haChaim tells us is that it is the fallen— those who have done damage—who are more important to our world. The people who are born good and stay good are nice people within whose lives the Opponent is not very strong; they will not elevate our world to its ultimate level. But the people for whom the Opponent is strong in their lives, those who fall— those are the people who have a chance to bring transformation.

The Ohr haChaim continues, "The Light that we receive is dependent on the difficulty of our work." And if the Opponent was even one degree weaker than he is, none of us would have the potential to achieve the ultimate level of *bilha hamavet lanetzach*, the total removal of pain and suffering from this world. So we have to remind ourselves that not only is the Opponent necessary, but the strength of the Opponent is also necessary. For where is the most Light revealed? Where the opposition to the Light is greatest.

THROUGH OUR STUDY WE CAN SEE EVERYTHING

By coming together, we will certainly reveal a certain amount of Light. But do you know when it's most important that we come together? When we do not want to come. When we do not want to pray. When we do not want to connect. Many of us think—especially those of us who've experienced *Rosh Hashanah, Yom Kippur, Sukkot*—that when we are excited about something, there is Light there, and of course, there is. But when can we reveal the most Light? When the Opponent is strongest. Sure, when the Opponent is allowing us to be enthusiastic, we will reveal some Light, but the real Light, the real growth will come when the Opponent fights harder! The stronger the Opponent, the greater and more powerful the Light we can reveal.

So when should we make our connections? Well, it is important always to make our connections, but we should definitely make them when we do not want to make them, when we do not want to share; when we do not want to inspire others. These are the opportunities in life to reveal the most Light.

In Beresheet, it also says: *"In creating our world, The Creator saw the Light that it was good."* The *Midrash* explains that the first Light that was revealed in our world shone for thirty-six hours, and then it was concealed. It was concealed because the Creator was afraid that if it was revealed in our world all the time, the Light would be taken and used for negative ends.

The Baal Shem Tov tells us, "Therefore, this Light was hidden." It's called the *Or HaGanuz* (Concealed Light). This is the Light that has within it the totality of Light, and life, and revelation, and fulfillment. The Baal Shem Tov said, "Where is that Concealed Light—which is called the *Or HaGanuz*, the

Light that was too great to be left in our world—concealed? It was concealed in the Torah."

There are many stories where we learn that the kabbalists, including the Baal Shem Tov, had the ability—through their reading of the Torah and specifically their reading of the *Zohar* —to see everything. We have to understand that each one of us is meant to attain this level, where, through our study, we can see everything—in the Torah, in the *Zohar*, even in the most mundane things.

Story: The Oxen

There is a story about one of the students of the Baal Shem Tov, Rav Baruch of Kaminka, who was an ox trader. One day, he sent some of his oxen to the market to be sold. He was afraid, however, because at that time, many of the animal traders who sent their animals to the market to be sold had the animals stolen. Rav Baruch was worried that his oxen might also be stolen, so he sent his son, Rav Josef, to ask the Baal Shem Tov what they should do. What could they do to keep his oxen safe? I enjoy the mundane aspect of this story: Rav Josef was not asking about his spiritual work. He was not asking about Light. He was asking about his father's oxen.

The Baal Shem Tov told Rav Josef, "You should have come to me before your father sent your oxen to be sold; then I could have ensured that they would be protected." With that the Baal Shem Tov opened the *Zohar* and started to read, and soon said to Rav Josef, "I see that your oxen have not been stolen." Rav Josef astonished, asked the Baal Shem Tov, "The oxen, my father's oxen, are all right? It says that in the *Zohar*?"

The Baal Shem Tov replied, "This is what it says in this week's story of Beresheet: The Creator saw that the Light was good, it was powerful, and He hid the Light in the Torah. And where specifically are the secrets of the Torah hidden? In the *Zohar*.

"With the Light that is called Concealed Light, you can see everything: everything that there was; everything that there is, and everything that there will be. If a person merits, through his study, to connect to the *Or HaGanuz*, to the Concealed Light in the Torah, he will have the ability to see everything, everything in our world—the most spiritual *and* the most mundane."

The Baal Shem Tov then said to Rav Josef, "Do you think all I saw was the oxen?"

Whenever awareness is achieved it is because this specific Light was revealed on the Shabbat of Beresheet. Every single one of us should awaken a desire on this Shabbat to be able to see, because every single one of us has the potential, with the gift of the *Zohar*, to see everything.

As the *Zohar* says, there are those who can see and there are those who cannot. Even those who can see do not have pure vision. But when we merit "seeing" through the *Zohar*, we see everything and our vision is pure. The revelation of this Concealed Light occurs for us on the

Shabbat of Beresheet. With, and because of, our connection to the *Zohar*, every single one of us, to one degree or another can merit truly seeing.

We have to awaken the desire (not only on the Shabbat of Beresheet but every time we open the *Zohar*), to study the *Zohar* and to try to understand what is being said there. We also need to realize that there are endless levels to the *Zohar*, including the physical, the spiritual, and the Supernal. Sometimes, vision will manifest as clearly as it did for the Baal Shem Tov. For some of us, it will come as an awakening of the heart, so that the next time we have a decision to make, we will have a little bit more insight because of the gift of vision that we received from the *Zohar*. Every single one of us needs to know that this gift to truly see is here for us, specifically on the Shabbat of Beresheet.

In his *Introduction to Ten Luminous Emanations* Rav Ashlag gives a long explanation of this teaching of the Baal Shem Tov. The Light of the Creation of our world (the Light that contains everything within itself), is concealed in the *Zohar*. Each one of us, to whatever degree we can, has the potential to use the Light to truly see—to see our lives now, to see our lives in the future, to see everything. But we have to ask for this ability: On the Shabbat of Beresheet, when that Light is being concealed in the *Zohar*, we need to seek, through our connection to the *Zohar*, to gain a greater and greater aspect of this true sight. It is a tremendous gift, and one that we must first desire and request before we can begin receiving it.

PERFECTION EXISTS HERE AND NOW

The last idea that I would like to share comes from the *Midrash*, from the section that speaks about the process of Creation, "*vayechulu hashamayim veha'aretz,*" which literally means "the Heavens and the Earth, [or the process of Creation], became complete." The word *vayechulu* means "completion," the perfection of that Creation.

The *Midrash* uses a parable to explain this statement. In Rome, some bath houses contained huge, beautiful baths whose floors were decorated with elaborate artwork. If the water in the bath was filthy, you would see nothing but filthy water. However, once you removed the filthy water the beauty of the artwork at the bottom of the bath stood revealed in all its glory. The *Midrash* explains that this example describes the process of Creation itself, where the world was completely in darkness, a darkness (*tohu vavohu*) that was like the dirty water in the bath. Nothing new needed to happen for Creation to take place—all that was required was the removal of the dirty water, or in this case, the removal of the darkness. The process of Creation was not a process of creating something new. It was a process of taking away the garbage so that the beauty of what was already there could be seen.

This is also true of our world today. The *Midrash* says that if we repeat the phrase, "*vayechulu hashamayin ve ha'aretz*", we can connect to this perfection that still exists, thus becoming a partner in the Creation of our world. What does this mean?

This is one of the most important lessons for our lives. All the illusion of pain, of suffering, even of death is just that—an illusion. It is filthy water in a beautiful bath. The beautiful artwork in the bath exists, but filthy water keeps us from seeing it. We have to know that it is here—that this perfection exists here and now. Rabbi Israel of Koznitz explains that there is going to come a time when we will look back and realize that this perfection was right here in front of us, right here all along.

When we have achieved our spiritual goals, most of us think that the world is going to change or that something new will appear in our lives. This is not going to happen. It is only that the veils—the dirty water—will be removed. To the degree that we are able to awaken the consciousness that perfection already exists for the world and for ourselves, we will experience that perfection.

Yes, as with the bath, there is probably some dirty water covering this perfection, but we do not need to create a perfect self. That perfect self already exists. The only work that we have to do (which was also the work of the Creation of our world) is to remove the filth and see the beauty that is revealed. Once we are aware that this is the reality, this consciousness overrides everything: what we think about ourselves, what we think about our world, what we think about what occurs in our lives. To the degree that we awaken this consciousness we can bring an end to pain, suffering, and death in our world. It is this consciousness of perfection that has to overtake our world.

Perfection is here now. Don't be fooled by the filthy water covering the artwork. Just remove it. No matter what happens in our lives, no matter what somebody does to us, no matter what we think of ourselves, perfection exists now. If we think that we are lacking and that the world is lacking and that therefore we have to create something new, we will never get there. We will never achieve our completion, nor will the world ever achieve its completion. We have to know clearly that perfection exists now. We are perfect. The perfection of the world is here now. Our work is simply to remove the illusion that tells us otherwise.

The *Midrash* explains that when pain, suffering, and death are finally removed from our world, the result will not be something new. It will be like looking all over the house for our glasses or our keys, when suddenly, we come back to our desk to find that what we were looking for was sitting right there all the time. It was there, we just did not see it. This is what it will be like.

The *Midrash* says (and this is one of my favorite verses): Change will occur in an instant. How can change occur in an instant if so much has to change in our world? Change can occur in an instant because perfection is already here. My perfection is here. Your perfection is here. Yes, there is work to be done to remove the filth that covers up the perfection, but the perfection is already here.

Our work is simply to strengthen this consciousness and awareness, which will consequently give us the strength and the impetus to clean out all the "filthy water"—to truly see and be shown the perfection that already exists.

Noach

"YOU SHOULD HAVE CRIED BEFORE"

I am always joyful when I have an opportunity to share insights of the *Zohar* that are not commonly read. There is a discussion in the *Hashmatot haZohar* (the sections that were not found by the first printing of the *Zohar*, but were later found and printed, and are called the omitted or missing *Zohar*) referring to the story of Noach that is important and beautiful.

The *Zohar* explains that when Noah came out of the ark and witnessed the destruction of the world, he began to cry. We cannot even begin to imagine his pain. If, God forbid, there were a nuclear war and you were the only survivor, you might have comparable feelings as you step out into the world, only to see millions of people and all other living things dead, to witness terrible destruction wherever you look.

Noah was a caring person. Yet the Creator said to Noah, "*Now* you have become awakened? *Now* you are crying? Noah, did you not understand that the reason I came before you and spoke those numerous times prior the flood was not because I loved you so much. The reason I spoke to you was to awaken in you the desire to beg for the world. When I said, 'Everyone in the world is negative; you are the only righteous person,' I did not intend to tell you how great you are. I came before you so that you could begin to do something for the world. When I spoke to you and said that I would bring destruction upon the world and instructed you to make yourself the ark, *that* is when you should have cried. The reason I kept returning to you was so you would understand that it was up to you to beg for mercy for the world. Yet when you understood that you were going to be saved, you did not ask for mercy for the world. All you did was make the ark and you were saved. Now that the world is destroyed, now you open up your mouth? Now you are begging? What are you begging for now?"

One of the purposes of a sacrifice is to atone, to help remove the darkness from a particular action. Once Noah realized his mistake, he brought a sacrifice to the Creator—as atonement for ignoring the Creator all the times He had come to Noah prior to the flood. Clearly, what the Creator was telling him was that he should have done all of his crying and all of his caring for the world *before* the destruction by the flood, not after.

In the *Zohar*, Rabbi Yochanan said: "Let us talk about the difference between Noah and the righteous people who came after him. Noah did not try to protect his generation. He did not pray for them like Abraham. Before the destruction of Sodom and Gomorrah, the Creator said to Abraham, 'The people are doing terrible things. There will be great destruction.' Abraham immediately begged the Creator not to destroy Sodom and Gomorrah. He asked the Creator, 'If there are forty righteous people in these towns combined, will You avert the destruction?' Abraham continued to beg that the towns be spared until he was down to only ten righteous people, and then requested of the Creator, 'Then save the towns for them.'" As an aside, it is interesting to note that in the Bible story, once Abraham had dropped to ten righteous people, he departed from the Creator. When you read this literally it means that Abraham, in effect, concluded, "If there are fewer than ten people, the towns will not be saved. So there is no point asking." However, the *Zohar* explains this differently: The *Zohar* states the reason Abraham stopped at ten is because he actually thought that there were ten righteous people in these towns and that he had been successful in his plea. That is why Abraham went away at this time. The main point I wish to make here is that even though Abraham did not succeed in preventing the destruction, he did everything he could until he thought he had succeeded.

After the Israelites sinned by making the golden calf, the Creator said to Moses, "Let me destroy them," and Moses immediately began praying. He was unrelenting in his prayer and thus protected his generation. The *Zohar* says that Moses spoke to the Creator and said, "You are called merciful. You should be merciful towards Your Creation. How can You allow this destruction to occur?" And he pleaded with the Creator,

"Take my life here in this world. Take my life in the next world. I will have nothing, but save them. Erase me from Your Book." Taken literally, this last statement appears to mean: Do not make me a leader anymore and take me out of the Torah. However, the *Zohar* explains that what Moses meant was: "Leave me here with nothing. Take away everything that I have in this world. Take away everything that I have in the next world." The *Zohar* tells us that the Israelites would have been destroyed, if not for Moses' prayerful appeals to the Creator to avert their destruction.

We have here three examples: Abraham, who begged but was not successful; Moses, who begged and was successful; and Noah, who did not beg.

In the *Zohar*, Rabbi Yeshua asks: "Why did Noah not pray?" We know Noah was a righteous person, regardless of the commentary and the questions raised about the level of his righteousness. Noah did not pray because he believed that perhaps he would be destroyed with them. Noah knew that he was not much better than everyone else. In fact, the *Midrash* explains that Noah needed the purification of the flood almost as much as the rest of his generation. But because he was enclosed in the ark, he was protected from the death and destruction. This teaches us that even if, God forbid, a person is deserving of experiencing the same judgment as the rest of the world, by "encircling" himself or herself with the Light of the *Zohar*, that person will receive protection.

We see from this lesson in the *Zohar* that Noah did not pray because he realized that he was not much better than anyone else. To clarify this point, consider the following example.

A person with very poor credit approaches a wealthy man to ask for a loan. Even though the wealthy man is aware that this individual has bad credit, he agrees to lend him the money. Then another borrower comes along who has an even more challenging credit situation than the first person. The first borrower pleads with the wealthy man to also give this new person a loan. It is now likely that the wealthy man is not only going to refuse to lend the second borrower money, he will more than likely ask the first person to return the money that was just loaned him, having lost confidence in the first borrower.

This was Noah's concern. Noah knew that he was skating on very thin ice. Although the Creator had said, "I will save you," Noah wanted to hide because he believed that if God should think about saving him for one more second, he, too, would be killed. The reason Noah did not want to pray and ask for mercy for the world was because he felt that he himself did not truly deserve to be saved either.

We have been examining the decisions of Noah, Abraham, and Moses, yet on one level, this comparison is not a fair one. Abraham was a very righteous person, and Moses was one of the highest souls that ever came to this world. Noah, however, was not on their level of righteousness. In the *Zohar*, Rav Elazar says: "Noah knew that he did not deserve to live. It was from Noah's piety, from his righteousness, that he believed that he should not ask." It was not that Noah did not care. Of course, he cared, but he knew that he could not make a difference because he did not deserve to ask.

THE DESIRE FOR OTHERS TO HAVE GOOD

The *Zohar* says (and this is something I regard as key): "The Creator loves, desires, and is connected to a person who asks for good things for others." How do we know this? In the Book of Judges, (chapters 6 through 8), we read how God chose Gideon, a young man from an otherwise unremarkable clan of the tribe of Manasseh, to free the people of Israel and condemn their worship of idols. Gideon was not righteous, nor were his parents, but because he asked for goodness for the Israelites, the Creator said to him, "You have all the power, all the Light you need to save them with the goodness that you wanted to bring down." What Light did Gideon have? What strength did he have? It was not his connection. It was not his wisdom. It was not the result of his actions. It was nothing. Gideon had no Light of his own, but because he desired good for the Israelites, the Creator gave him all the power he needed. This is an amazing lesson.

What the *Zohar* tells us (and what Noah did not understand) is that even if we are evil, even if we have no Light, no special claim to virtue, as long as we truly have a desire to help another person, that desire will connect us to the Creator and will give us all the strength and Light that we need to provide that help. This is an enlightening revelation.

Often when we're trying to help people, we question ourselves: "How strong are we? How much do we know? What gives us the right to help?" It is true that most of us do not have enough wisdom, or enough connection to the Light of the Creator, or, for that matter, any reason why we should be able to help others, yet from the examples of Gideon and Noah, we learn this powerful lesson: We do not need anything—not wisdom, not even the Light. We do not need to be good people. All we need is to have is a pure desire to help the other person. As the *Zohar* tells us: If we have a true desire to help the other person—even if we are not worthy, even if we are not right—we can still be the conduit to help another.

What an empowering understanding. This is what the Creator told Noah. "You missed the mark. It was not that you were righteous. It was not that you could have saved the world through your work, or that you deserved to ask that the world be saved. But if you had had a true desire to help another person, to help the world, that one desire and nothing else—with no Light behind it, no wisdom behind it, no action behind it—would have given you the strength to change the world."

This is a concept that I find unbelievably inspiring. The *Zohar* tells us that Gideon had no right to help; he had no right to save the Israelites. Gideon was not righteous; he had no positive actions; he had no wisdom; and he had no real connection to the Light of the Creator that would give him that right. Yet because Gideon had a simple desire to help the Israelites and he wanted to do good for them, the Creator said, "Go with that power."

What does this mean in terms of our work in this world, our work with other people? We do not have to have anything or be anyone of any importance; all we need is a true desire to share. When there is someone in our life—someone we speak with, even someone we have just come across—we may very well have the wisdom or the connection to help him or her, or for whatever reason we may be a little bit more connected than they are; although it is a great asset or support to have this wisdom, it is not the wisdom itself that will provide the help this person needs. It is very important for us to understand that even when we think that we have the Light or the wisdom to help (and indeed, may actually have the Light or the wisdom that can help), there is a greater, more important, more effective way to help another person, and that is a true desire on our part for them to "have good." If we have a true desire for that person to have good, then we are not giving of ourselves. This is an enormously inspiring lesson.

A true desire for another person to "have good" is a practical tool for making a difference in someone's life. This is how we can change the world. This is what the Creator was saying to Noah. Do you think Noah did not cry for the world? Of course, he cried for the world. Did Noah not try to do what he could? Of course, he tried to do what he could. But Noah did not understand this concept: that it was not that there was something he himself could do, nor did he need to be connected or need to reveal Light, all Noah had to do was to awaken this true desire to help the world.

The *Midrash* explains that when Abraham begged the Creator, he asked, "How can You use judgment? If You want the world to survive, You cannot come with judgment. If You do not forgive a little bit, the world will not be sustained." The Creator said to Abraham, "I see that you are a man who always works to bring charity and righteousness to the world. I also see that you want to bring righteousness for the protection of humanity, and you do not want judgment to come upon them." The *Midrash* says it was at this moment—when Abraham said to the Creator, "I want only goodness to come to the world; I do not want judgment to come down to this world"—that Abraham achieved his spiritual level. The *Midrash* goes on to explain that this is why Abraham was chosen and anointed above all other righteous people. (We also sing such praise for Rabbi Shimon bar Yochai, the author of the *Zohar*). The *Midrash* tells us that the Creator said to Abraham the Patriarch, "You are chosen from your friends. There have been ten generations from Noah until you, Abraham. Of all those generations, I want to talk only to you. I have no desire to be connected to or to talk to anybody else. That is why you, Abraham, are chosen above everyone who ever lived from the time of Noah until your time."

Abraham was not chosen because of his righteousness, or because of all the good that he did for other people. Abraham was anointed because of his desire for goodness to come down to this world.

We do not have enough of this desire. To awaken a stronger and stronger desire for goodness to come down to this world is something separate and apart from the rest of our spiritual work. We can change the world; we can save the world. We can change a person; we can save a person. But to achieve this, we have to be like Gideon; constantly awakening in ourselves a stronger and stronger desire to help others, as well as understanding that it will be from this desire alone— not from our wisdom or our spiritual connection—that we can and will help people.

Why was Abraham chosen, why was he anointed more than anyone who ever lived? The *Midrash* tells us it was not because of Abraham's level of connection, it was not due to his level of spiritual elevation. It was simply because Abraham wanted to bring goodness to this world and he did not want judgment to come down to this world.

This is something all of us can do. Will we achieve the level of Abraham, or Noah, or Gideon? I don't know. But we certainly can grow our desire that goodness come to another person, and also grow our desire that goodness come to the world. When we truly awaken and understand the power of desiring good for others, this will give us the strength to do anything. It's an amazing lesson.

NOT TO ACCEPT JUDGMENT

The third lesson I would like to share concerns the question: Why did Noah not pray? Noah did not pray because he realized that the judgment of the flood was signed, sealed, and given over. But one of the things that my father, the Rav is always clear about is that no matter how final something is, we never accept it. One of the mistakes Noah made was that once he deemed that the flood was imminent, he thought there was nothing more he could do. "Let me at least save myself so that humanity can continue." However, what we have to learn from the story of Noach is that we should never accept anything as final. Never accepting is a shift in consciousness that is remote for many of us, but it is something we need to develop.

There is a beautiful story from the *Talmud* in *Tractate Brachot* that illustrates this idea.

King Hezekiah became ill, and it appeared that he was going to die. Isaiah the Prophet came to him and said, "The Creator has sent me to tell you that you are going to die; you will not live." Now this was not a doctor's diagnosis—this was God talking through Isaiah. Isaiah then told the king, "Put your affairs in order because you are going to die; you are not going to live." Initially, it just seems as if God told the king that he was going to die physically. But what does "You are going to die; you will not live" mean? Why the redundancy? God sent this message twice to say: "You are going to die soon physically, *and* in the next world. God wants you to know you are going to die in a little while. This life is over, and just so you understand, you have nothing in the next world either."

Obviously, the king was just a little bit shaken up by this news. The king asked Isaiah, "What is happening here?" Now at this point in King Hezekiah's life, he did not have children. We know, God forbid, that sometimes, for whatever reason, people cannot have children. But in King Hezekiah's case, he had never tried to have children. The Creator was not saying that the king was being punished for not having children, but that he was being punished for not even *trying* to have children.

King Hezekiah explained, "But you must know that I did not have children because I foresaw with *Ruach HaChodesh* (Divine Inspiration) that if I have children, they will be negative; they will be evil. I would rather not have children and not bring more evil people into this world." Isaiah the Prophet responded, "Why are you worrying about Divine Inspiration?"

Throughout history, there have been people who like to meet with psychics to gain knowledge about what is going to happen in the future. But there is a danger in doing that. Firstly, what the psychics say is often not true, and secondly, even if what they say is true, we have to live our lives with the understanding that we have the power to change anything and everything at any given moment.

When a person hears a prediction through Divine Inspiration, this is more reliable than a prediction from a psychic. King

Hezekiah, therefore, knew this prediction was true—that if he were to have children, they were going to be evil. He saw this through Divine Inspiration and he knew it to be a fact, and yet Isaiah the Prophet told him that he should not be worrying about the future in this way. Isaiah said to the king, "What you need to do, you need to do; and whatever God's plans are, let Him take care of that. You need to worry only about what you need to do to take care of it."

So King Hezekiah replied to Isaiah, "Okay, so let me marry your daughter. Maybe because of my merit and your merit together, your daughter and I will have righteous children." Isaiah answered, "No wedding. The judgment is done. You're going to die."

King Hezekiah was upset with Isaiah's response and therefore, did not address him by his name, saying instead, "Son of Amoz, stop your prophecy and leave. This is a teaching I received from my great-grandfather: Even if the sword is already at the throat, we should not stop asking for mercy from the Creator. Even at that moment—a second before a person dies—they must know with certainty that they do not have to die, that everyone can change his or her destiny."

Again, we are not speaking about a doctor's diagnosis in this story. It was God who told King Hezekiah that he was going to die. But the king refused to accept that judgment. And here we can see Noah's mistake. When God came to him and said, "It is over; the only hope now for humanity is that you survive and have children," Noah thought, "If God says it is over, it is over." But the lesson here for us is that no, it is never over. Never, never, never accept a final decree!

Noah, however, can still correct this mistake. Every year, on the Shabbat when we read the story of Noach, Noah comes back to us and gives us the strength to change this consciousness of accepting finality. As I said previously, "Nothing is ever final, ever" is, and has always been, a driving force for my father, the Rav. If God sends His prophet to you and the prophet says you are to die, do not accept it. If God comes to you and says the world is going to end, do not accept it.

For many of us who are so far away from this understanding, we have to work towards having a consciousness of accepting nothing, of never giving up. By not accepting, we can—and will—change everything.

Lech Lecha

ARE WE BATTLING ALL THE TIME?

When I teach or study about Abraham, I am always inspired. Of the three patriarchs—Abraham, Isaac, and Jacob—Abraham was the first true revolutionary. When God put Adam on the Earth, God advised Adam about what needed to be done. During the time of Noach, even though the world was in turmoil, remnants still remained of the secrets revealed to Adam by the angel Raziel. However, from the time of Adam to the time of Abraham humanity fell spiritually, so God did not communicate with Abraham the way He had communicated with Adam or with Noach before the Flood. Abraham's awakening occurred because of his own desire to be awakened. Abraham was the first person in the world to understand that we need to awaken our desire on our own to connect to the Light of the Creator.

How do we know if we are truly connected to the wisdom of Kabbalah? If, God forbid, there was no Kabbalah Centre, or other place of spiritual study in the world, would we fight for it? Would we make it our life's goal to ensure that there would be a Kabbalah Centre or spiritual place of study in the world and would we strive tirelessly to spread the wisdom of Kabbalah to the world? This is what Abraham did. In his time, there was nothing—no Light. Abraham realized that to draw the Light he had to awaken a desire within himself. Abraham fought and fought, and at times was even willing to give up his life to bring the Light of the Creator to the world.

There is so much to appreciate and learn from Abraham. In the *Talmud: Sanhedrin*, where the sages discuss the patriarchs, they speak specifically about Abraham and the story of Lech Lecha. The Creator said to Abraham, "*Lech lecha* (you go). (Genesis 12:1) "You go" implies constant motion—to be in a constant battle, which is what life is all about. This constant motion is what a real spiritual connection with the Creator is all about.

Someone who is really connected to the Light of the Creator has this quality of constant motion within him- or herself. How did the Creator perceive Abraham? What is it about Abraham that made the Creator happy? The *Midrash* says the Creator called Abraham "yedidi" (My best friend) and *"Avraham ohavi"* (Abraham, My beloved). What was is it about Abraham that made the Creator feel this way about him? Just as there are certain qualities you identify with in someone that makes that individual your best friend, what was it about Abraham that made him *ohavi* (My beloved) and *yedidi*

(My best friend) for the Creator? The Creator connected to Abraham so strongly because Abraham viewed his life as a constant struggle.

The *Midrash* explains that Abraham had achieved the level expressed by the metaphor that he ran against the rapids in front of a herd of wild horses chasing him from behind.

Abraham merited being *Avraham ohavi* and *yedidi*, the best friend of the Creator, because he viewed his life as this constant struggle—running and pushing against the rapids. This is a lesson we have to learn. This is the way we have to view our spiritual work. We need to constantly ask ourselves: Are we at least *trying* to be like Abraham in this sense? Are we battling all the time, pushing all the time? The example above is very clear. Doing our spiritual work in a relatively calm and easy manner, battling every once in a while, is certainly not how we should aspire to be like Abraham. To be like Abraham is to ask ourselves: "What am I doing to push myself, to throw myself into the rushing water? Am I willing to run and run and run as the raging waters thrash against me?" This was the consciousness of Abraham. The Creator said, "This is the quality of Abraham that made Me love him, the quality of Abraham that made him close to Me."

Most of us are far from having this kind of consciousness. Every so often, we will battle; every once in a while, we will do something to push ourselves. But to be constantly living our lives like Abraham—running against the rapids while the horses chase us for miles upon miles—is something we need to ask for, something we need to desire. If we don't ask for it, if we don't desire it, we will never get there. But how many of us even desire this: to be running against the rapids?

I think most of us would probably be overwhelmed just by the thought of doing this. However, it is important to at least ask the Creator, "I realize how weak I am, and that I probably cannot run against the rapids, but I'm asking You, I'm begging You, please give me the strength to be like Abraham. This is what I want. I do not want my life to be easy. I do not want my spiritual work to be easy. I know I am very far from this consciousness. I know that I would have the strength to handle this if You gave it to me today. But this is what I want. I want my work to be difficult work, and I want to have the strength to do it. I want to be like Abraham, constantly running against the rapids, all the time, every day of my life. Please give me that strength."

If we keep this consciousness as our goal, the Creator will give us assistance. Unfortunately, most of us are very far from even asking for this consciousness, far from even desiring this connection with the Creator. This consciousness begins with the understanding that this is what we want our spiritual life to be like. Each Shabbat, when we read about Abraham, this quality of Abraham is available for us to request. Specifically, on the Shabbat of Lech Lecha, Abraham comes to us and gives us this strength. The desire to have the strength to push ourselves against the current changes the intention of our spiritual work, changes what we desire from our spiritual work. Abraham comes to us and we can ask him to give us the strength to be a little bit like him.

Most of us would like our spiritual life to be an endless connection to the Creator. Every morning when we wake up and meditate or pray we desire to feel the Creator. As we go about our day, we want to feel the Creator. When we read or scan the *Zohar*, it is with the intention of connecting to the Creator and to Rabbi Shimon bar Yochai. This, however, was not what Abraham sought, and it is not what we should desire either.

It is imperative that we understand that we came to this world to work hard. In *Ten Luminous Emanations*, Rav Ashlag explains the concept of *bameitim chofshi* (the only time a person is free from this struggle is when he is dead). While we are in this world, we need to constantly be asking for our lives to be a struggle. Not the kind of struggle where we have doubts all the time, or the daily dramas that most of us view as struggles. Those are not what we are talking about here. Can you imagine Abraham waking up every day and saying, "Oh, I am so depressed, this is so difficult."? No, Abraham was excited to wake up each day and push himself. This consciousness gave him his connection with the Creator and filled him with Light of the Creator.

This desire does not mean that we are asking the Creator that every day be overwhelming. What it means is having the consciousness to ask the Creator for the strength, desire, and enthusiasm to push every day. That is what our lives need to be about. We have to ask ourselves, "Do I understand this to be my singular desire?" and really think about it. For many of us, to ask for our lives to be a struggle would be a dramatic shift. To want our life—from the moment we wake up in morning till we go to bed at night—to be as if we are running against the rapids, to be like Abraham and think, "This struggle makes me the happiest person in the world."

There were very few souls—possibly Moses is the only one—who came close to the level of joy that Abraham felt every day. No greater fulfillment can come to us than being of this consciousness. In truth, this is the purpose of our spiritual work. As Rav Ashlag says, *"Bemeitim chofshi,"* (the only time a person is free from this struggle is when he is dead). If a person, God forbid, is spiritually dead in our world, he has this fake rest now. But our desire should be to fight—to wake up every morning and feel the struggle against the current. This desire to fight offers the greatest fulfillment. This is the level of Abraham.

Story: Not Wanting the Angel

Many people throughout history had angels that came and taught them. Rabbi Josef Karo was such a man. However, when the angels approached the Gaon of Vilna (Rabbi Eliyahu ben Shlomo Zalman, 1720- 1797) because they wanted to teach him wisdom, he replied, "I do not want you to teach me. I want to struggle for the wisdom; I want to work for it."

How many of us could conceive such a thing? If an angel came to teach us wisdom, how many of us would turn that angel away and say, "No, I want to fight for it, I want to struggle for it."? This is the level of Abraham.

This sense of excitement for "the struggle" is the message that permeates the Shabbat of Lech Lecha. First, we need to understand that this is what we should desire our life to be. Second, it is important to have clarity that the eagerness we should feel for the struggle does not mean that our life will always be overwhelming, but rather that we have sense of enthusiasm for the struggle, for the fight, for the run against the current. The desire for the struggle is not depressing. It is invigorating, it is exhilarating, it is inspiring—it is the gift of Abraham on the Shabbat of Lech Lecha.

"GOD, OPEN UP MY MOUTH"

The Talmud asks, "What should a person in this world do?" And the Talmud answers, "A person in this world should act like a mute." The *Ma'or Einayim* (Rav Menachem Nachum of Chernobyl 1730 - 1797) says that we should ask "*HaShem sefatai tiftach* (God, open up my mouth)," which is from Psalms 51:17. Ultimately, we must come to the point where we truly understand, know, and desire not to have any power of speech; where we do not want to speak any words on our own, where we want to be mute except when the Creator wants us to say something. When the Creator wants us to open up our mouths, we want Him to talk through us.

On a spiritual level, when we teach somebody, we should understand that asking the Creator to speak through us must be a constant consciousness that becomes second nature to us. Before we teach or advise someone, before we share spiritual lessons, we should stop for a second and say, *"HaShem sefatai tiftach,"* and think, "I do not want to speak; I do not have the power to speak." The first step for us is to truly understand that we do not have the ability to do anything. We do not have the ability to speak, we do not have the ability to teach, and we do not have the ability to give anyone assistance with our mouth.

Most of us, however, to some degree or another, think it is *we* who are talking when *we* begin speaking. Right? We think *we* are teaching, and *we* are doing something that can help. But what should we truly do? Before we speak, we should think to ourselves, "I am a mute, I have no ability to speak. I have no ability to share, no ability to give wisdom, no ability to give advice. *HaShem sefatai tiftach* (God, please let Your words come through me)." First we need to have the true understanding that we have no ability with our mouth. Indeed, this understanding has to be complete and clear, but for most of us it is not. Once this is clear, we can then ask the Creator to open up our mouths to speak, and then the Creator will speak through us.

Furthermore, the *Ma'or Einayim* says that this holds true not only when we are studying or when we are teaching. We should know that whatever we say is the Word of the Creator coming through us. This should be our consciousness, even if we are speaking about mundane things like giving directions to someone, because everything in our world—even the most ordinary of things—is really of the Creator. Therefore, the next level of our understanding is that we should know, even when we are speaking of mundane things, that it is the Creator talking through us.

This level of understanding is so important for us to reach. Ideally, even when we're walking down the street and somebody asks us for directions, we should think to ourselves that we cannot be the one to give him the directions. We cannot speak; we want the Creator to speak through us. Even if someone calls us up to ask about the weather, our consciousness should be: "I cannot speak, I'm an *ilem* (mute), but the Creator can speak through me."

I am not sure if we all want to focus on this second level—to realize that everything that we verbalize, even the most mundane of things, comes from the Creator—right away. The first level, however—being a mute with regard to spiritual matters, is so very important. As the *Talmud* asks: "What should a person do all the time in this world?" This is not simply a good lesson, but this should actually be the way we live our lives. Certainly if we are teaching, if we are saying words that we want other people to be assisted by, our first step is to say, "No, I know that in this world, I am a mute," meaning of course we can speak words, but nothing we say can have any influence; nothing we say can give any long-term assistance. If we really comprehend this—and it takes work to arrive at this awareness—then we can ask *"HaShem sefatai tiftach,"* (God, open up my mouth so that whatever I say will be of You). This is a very important consciousness to reach.

There are stories of kabbalists who, while speaking about the most mundane of matters, were really hinting at codes concerning the Supernal Worlds. Students of theirs, who understood the way of spiritual work, would realize that there were secrets, hints, and codes concerning the Supernal Worlds in everything that their teachers were saying.

Story: Talking to the Cook in Prayer

There is a famous story of a great kabbalist who stopped right in the middle of his prayers, walked into the kitchen and had a fifteen-minute conversation with the cook. The kabbalist was praying *Shacharit*, the morning prayers, and had donned his *Talit* (prayer shawl) and his *Tefillin* (phylacteries). Suddenly, his students witnessed him walk towards the kitchen, stop his prayers in a place where one is not supposed to speak, enter the kitchen and start to ask the cook about what she was making and the ingredients she was using. Some of his students became very upset: They could not fathom how their teacher, in the middle of his prayers could just stop praying and start talking to the cook about breakfast. However, other students who had a little more insight were able to observe how the entire conversation was really about secrets concerning the Supernal Worlds.

Most of us are not at this level yet. However, we can begin working on it right away by becoming aware of how we should be in this world—of knowing that we have no speech, and of always, always, always asking the Creator *"HaShem sefatai tiftach."* The Creator will come into our mouths only when we have accomplished the first step—when we have clarity that we ourselves cannot say anything of consequence that can help in the long-term.

OUR PERSONAL SPIRITUAL WORK
AFFECTS OTHER SOULS

The third lesson I would like to share is a very important teaching for all of us who are involved in the work of assisting the souls of our world. The Torah says that when Abraham and Sarah left for the land of Canaan, they took all the souls that they had made in Haran with them. (*Genesis 12:5*) When we assist a soul, when we elevate a soul, we receive part ownership in that soul. This is a very important understanding for us with regards to the work that we do. Abraham and Sarah owned those souls that they brought out from Haran and connected to the Light of the Creator. They received some ownership of them and, therefore, received a lot of Light from those souls that they had made. With God's help, may all of us, in the work that we do, make souls every day.

The *Ma'or Einayim* says that every soul in our world has a connection to the Torah. This means there is a cable that goes from our personal work and study—both in the wisdom that we study and in the spiritual work that we do—to other people in the world. When we study and do our spiritual work we elevate all the souls that are connected through this work.

Abraham, through the spiritual tools that he used and through his personal work, elevated not just himself but all the souls that were connected to the Light of the Torah. These other souls elevated a little with Abraham, and because of this elevation, they came to Abraham and asked him to teach them.

This is a very important understanding. We have to always remember that when we help and teach people, our personal internal spiritual elevation is very connected to the assistance that we give to others.

Obviously, Abraham was a great soul, who had an extraordinary connection to the souls of the world, but each one of us has connections to souls of our world. There are many people who are at a level where they either have no spiritual awakening at all or whatever spiritual awakening they have is limited but they are still tethered to us on our soul level. When we elevate a little, we elevate them a little as well. This elevation causes these souls to come to a place where they are a little more open spiritually. Sometimes, these souls will come to us for the first time, or if they had been connected to us previously, they become more open to us.

Why? What suddenly happens here? As with Abraham, because he elevated so high, all those other lower souls that were connected to him elevated a little higher as well, and this elevation helped them realize that they should come to Abraham and study from him. Therefore, we have to understand that all of the personal spiritual work that we do is what elevates and awakens the souls that are connected to us.

Every elevation that we experience lifts them up a little higher as well. They become more open; they become more able to understand. If we are not doing our spiritual work and elevating ourselves, these souls stay where they are. In that case, hopefully, something these souls are doing personally will awaken them. But if we want to truly assist the souls that are, in one way or another, connected to us, we have to be constantly elevating ourselves. The higher we elevate, the higher all those souls will elevate with us. Abraham's example should awaken this consciousness within us.

Abraham knew that no matter how great his soul was, he was not able to awaken the world. He was not able to teach people, to inspire people to make them want to change until he had first done his own spiritual work. But once he had elevated through his spiritual work, he could elevate those other souls a little as well, so that they would become awakened and desire to go to Abraham and study from him. If Abraham, no matter how great he was, no matter how connected to the Light he was, just tried to teach them, he would not have been able to elevate them. It was only once Abraham had done his own spiritual work and elevated himself, that all the souls that were tethered to him began awakening and elevating a little, too.

How did Abraham and Sarah have the ability to awaken all of those souls? It was because of their personal elevation as a result of their own spiritual work and their connection to others. Those souls, once elevated a little, became more open; they began having the desire to grow, to change, and to learn from Abraham.

The lesson for us is we cannot hope to help others, to elevate others, to teach others, if we are not personally elevating ourselves. The souls who are connected to us will stay at *their* level if we stay at *our* level. When we elevate a little higher, all those souls who are connected to us, who were previously closed, become open for us to do something for them. Suddenly, these souls will begin to understand something that they previously could not comprehend. We need to know that when this occurs, it is because of our personal work of elevating ourselves. With our elevation, we elevate all the souls that are connected to us. If we remain stuck, if we remain low, all the souls that are connected to us remain low as well. It would have been impossible for Abraham to help his generation, to help those souls that eventually came to study from him if he did not elevate himself first.

Remember, no matter how great Abraham was, no matter how wise or connected he was, it was impossible for him to help the people in his generation without doing his spiritual work first. Abraham had to elevated himself first, and then, as a result of that elevation, he could elevate those souls a little so that they would become awakened and want to study from him. This is a tremendously important lesson, one that we need to be very clear about. Without our own constant spiritual elevation the souls that are connected to us will remain stuck.

WE CAN REVEAL THE GREATEST LIGHT
BECAUSE WE ARE SO LOW

The Bible says that after the destruction of the cities of Sodom and Gomorrah, the daughters of Abraham's nephew, Lot, lay with their father and conceived children by him. The explanation given is that Lot's daughters believed that they and their father were the only remaining survivors in the world and that the act of lying with their father was the only hope for the continuation of humankind. The *Midrash* explains that Lot's daughters said, "We will make alive, from our father, a continuation, a (*zerah*) seed," and not, "We will have a child by our father."

Why did Lot's daughters use the word *zerah*, or "seed," rather than "child?" The daughters used the word "seed" to indicate that the action of lying with their father was not necessarily to have a child at that time but to accomplish something far greater: They were planting a seed for the future. The word "seed" signifies the manifestation of the soul of *Mashiach* (Messiah), the revelation of the Light of *bila hamavet lanetzach* (victory over death, or the death of death), and *Techiyat Hametim* (resurrection of the dead, or immortality).

It is important for us to know that *Mashiach* will not come from the best of circumstances. *Mashiach* will come from the lineage of a daughter who slept with her father and conceived a child. Why is the seed of *Mashiach* manifesting from such a lowly, coarse relationship? There must be something significant here for us to learn.

Rabbi Aharon of Karlin explains that after the sin of Adam, the Supernal Lights (sparks of Light) fell into the depths of the *klipot* (negative shells that engulf the Light), into the depths of the darkness. From the moment the sparks fell until the time when *Mashiach* will manifest in our world, the process of both our, and humanity's spiritual work is to cleanse, purify, and elevate these sparks of Light from the darkness. *Mashiach* will only appear once this process of purification is complete.

Now we can understand why the soul of King David (which is also the soul of *Mashiach*) had to come from a lineage that originated at the lowest of levels. The revelation of the *Gemar haTikkun* (Final Redemption) is dependent upon the elevation of the sparks in the lowest levels of the *klipot*. Therefore, the process of creating the seed for the soul of *Mashiach* in this world had to come from the lowliest relationship possible.

Rav Ashlag asks why the coming of *Mashiach* will take place in our generation. How is it possible that we will be able to accomplish what all the great souls like Abraham, Moses and Rabbi Shimon did not accomplish? Are we really going to be able to achieve something that they could not? The answer is yes! In spiritual terms, most of us are as lowly as the daughters of Lot, and thus, we, too, have the ability to elevate these sparks, to bring that *zerah*, that seed, to manifest *Mashiach*. Abraham could not, Moses could not, and Rabbi Shimon bar Yochai could not. But we can.

To achieve the revelation of the Light stuck in the lowest of levels, the lowest of people are required. This is why our generation can elevate the sparks of Light from the lowest levels of the *klipot*.

The sages teach that *Mashiach* can only come in a generation that is either entirely pure, or entirely negative. What does this mean? Our generation, because of its base quality, has the ability to elevate the sparks that have fallen to the lowest levels of the *klipot*.

The *Talmud* refers to a conversation between a great soul and the soul of a king who had reigned during the period when idol worship was rampant in the world. This great soul asked the king, "How were you able to follow and worship idols?" The king replied, "If you had been alive at that time, you would have been the first one in line." Idol worship is like any other desire. We all have lowly desires that we act upon in this world. The *Talmud* says that the souls at the time when idol worship was so prevalent eventually came together and asked the Creator to remove this intense desire from our world. As a result, idol worship, the strongest of these base desires at that time, was nullified at a certain point in history, which is why most of us today have no desire to worship idols. This does not mean that our generation is superior to those generations who worshiped idols; the sages of that era simply performed an action which removed the desire to worship idols from the world.

How did one eradicate the magnetic craving for the idols in the days when idols had power? The *Midrash* explains that only a person who had previously been an idol worshiper and then transformed back had the ability to remove the power from the idols. It is the same for us. According to the wisdom of Kabbalah, there are 320 sparks of Light that have to be elevated in our generation, and when we achieve the elevation of 288 out of the 320 sparks of Light, everything will change.

The Ari (Rav Isaac Luria) says we are at the heels of this purification process. We are literally at the bottom of the bottom of the bottom, and for the sparks at the bottom of the bottom of the bottom to be elevated we need souls that have a *shivui tzurah* (similarity of form) with the bottom of the bottom of the bottom.

Therefore, our generation has the ability to bring *Mashiach*, something no earlier generation could do. Although this sounds strange, it is very serious because the next time we fall spiritually, the next time we look at ourselves and know—if we are honest with ourselves—how low we are and we think, "How can I possibly imagine that I could help another person; how can I possibly dream that I can reveal Light?" the answer is that we can reveal this Light simply because we *are* so low. On the other hand, if we were elevated spiritually like Rabbi Shimon bar Yochai, we would have no essential function in this world.

I was once asked, "Why did Rav Ashlag leave this world? He was obviously able to control death, so why did he choose not to stay here?" The answer to this question has many levels. On one level, it makes sense that any true kabbalist, certainly in the time of the coming of *Mashiach*, would wish to spearhead the movement towards *bila hamavet lanetzach* (the removal of death). However, at some point in time, Rav Ashlag probably realized that for whatever reason, he was not going to be able to achieve *bila hamavet lanetzach* in his generation. Instead, Rav Ashlag assembled all that he could: He wrote books, he taught Rav Brandwein, and he laid down the seeds. In Rav Ashlag's mind, he was probably thinking, "I have done what I can do: the rest will be done by others."

On another level, it is possible that Rav Ashlag knew that it was not his job to bring *Mashiach*. Rav Ashlag was too elevated. He had to wait for people as low as our generation to bring *Mashiach*. Although this concept is difficult to digest, it is a very crucial point. The Opponent wants us to think about how low we are, meaning we cannot reveal and elevate these captured sparks of Light; and that it doesn't make any sense that we will be able to reveal Light, and that we will be able to teach. But in fact, not only does it make sense that we can reveal Light, we are, indeed, the only ones who can actually do the job. There is literally no generation better suited to this task of bringing *Mashiach*.

Anyone who is greater than we are, who is more elevated spiritually than we are, could not achieve this. Only because of where our generation is at spiritually can we finish the job. This is why the seed of *Mashiach* begins in a dirty, dark way. It is only from within the darkness that *Mashiach* can become truly manifest. This is an astonishing revelation.

BY REMOVING ALL SELFISH ATTACHMENTS WE CAN KEEP LOVE FOREVER

Next, I would like to share what I think are a few very inspiring lessons that we can learn from story of the *Akedah*, the Binding of Isaac. As mentioned previously, the Binding of Isaac is a powerful spiritual process that is reawakened within us every time we read the story of Vayera on Shabbat.

The *Midrash* says that the Creator came to Abraham and said, "Take your son and bring him as a sacrifice…" Abraham walked with Isaac for three days. They arrived at the mountain, Abraham prepared the wood, and he bound Isaac on the altar. There are many beautiful commentaries in the *Midrash* that speak about the process of the Binding.

Abraham took the knife and was about to kill his son when an angel said to him, "Do not kill Isaac." The *Midrash* says that Abraham spoke to the Creator at this point and said, "I have a big problem with You now, God. Some time ago, You told me Isaac would be my seed, that he would continue spreading this wisdom throughout the world. Next You came to me and said, 'Take your son and sacrifice him.' Now You are telling me not to kill him. What is going on?"

The Creator replied, "Abraham, I have never changed my mind, nor have I changed my words. When I said to you, 'Take your son,' I did not tell you to slaughter him. I told you to elevate him as a sacrifice; I did not say 'kill him.' You have done all I have requested of you; You brought Isaac to the altar; you bound him and lay him on the altar. Now take him down."

The *Midrash* explains that the Creator said to Abraham, "It was not that I said one thing and meant something else. You misunderstood, but My Word was always true." This is a very puzzling section of the Midrash.

The *Midrash* explains that as Abraham was walking with Isaac to perform the Binding, the Satan danced in front of him and asked him all kinds of questions, thus injecting doubt into his mind. Satan said to Abraham, "You think that God told you to take Isaac as a sacrifice, but it was not God, it was the negative side."

Abraham said to Satan, "I have complete certainty and clarity that it was the Creator Who spoke to me." If the message that

Abraham received from the Creator to kill Isaac was so clear that he had no doubt or uncertainty about it, then why then does the Creator now say that the Creator never meant for Abraham to kill Isaac?

Further, the *Midrash* writes: After the Creator told Abraham not to kill Isaac, Abraham presumably a little upset, said to the Creator, "If this is so, did I come here for nothing? Did I waste my time? At least, let me cut him a little bit; let a little bit of blood come out." The Creator replied, "Do not do anything to Isaac; do not cause any harm to him." This is astounding! After the Creator told Abraham not to kill Isaac, Abraham still wanted to do damage on his own. What purpose would it serve for Abraham to cut Isaac?

What does "Did I come here for nothing?" mean? Before I can answer this question, we have to understand the concept of thought and action. We know it is not enough to think, "Oh, I want to share, I want to teach, I want to do something." In our world thoughts alone are not enough. A positive spiritual action such as a thought does not reveal any Light as long as it remains just a thought. Thought reveals the Light only when it is manifested as an action.

For most of us, no matter how pure and how great our thoughts are, when we actually take action, the result is much more powerful than all of our prior thoughts.

When Abraham brought Isaac and put him on the altar, Abraham's thoughts were so real, so powerful, that in his mind he had already killed Isaac. Abraham's intention to completely detach from any selfish attachments that he felt toward his beloved son was so powerful and his desire to give Isaac to the Creator (whatever that means) so pure, that it felt to him as if he had already performed the action.

The *Akedat Yitzhak* is a story that we can all learn from. It is a story about lasting love, and about anything and everything of a lasting nature that we desire. Most of us, even in our positive attachments to our friends, and to the people we love, have a large element of selfishness, of *Desire to Receive for the Self Alone* injected into the relationship, which will eventually cause the love in the relationship to die. When a deadly poisonous snake bites a person, the effect might take some time to manifest itself, but once the venom has been injected it will inevitably cause death, if left untreated.

So no matter how pure our love is for another person, for our children, or for our friends, to the degree that there is selfishness attached to that love, the relationship will have to end. Unfortunately, for many people, it ends at death. However, there is a way to make a relationship, or a love death-proof, but to completely detach all selfish desires from a relationship is very difficult to achieve. For most of us it is impossible.

The Creator came to Abraham and said, "Do you want your relationship with Isaac to last forever, or do you want it to last only while you are alive in this world, another forty years, another sixty years, another eighty years? If you want your relationship with Isaac to last forever, give him up completely.

Only if you can bring yourself to give him up completely will your relationship with him be everlasting."

For most people, when someone tells us to stop a negative action or to give something up, we can convince ourselves in our imagination that we have accomplished the task. Imagine a person eating a steak who sees a friend who is really hungry. The individual gives the starving friend his steak. The hungry man does not want to eat his friend's steak, but he eats it anyway, just to give his friend pleasure.

Put yourself in the hungry man's shoes. You and I can try to convince ourselves that we will eat the steak only because it is going to give pleasure to our friend, but after the first piece of steak enters our mouth, or at least after the second piece, our selfish nature will almost certainly kick in and we will start to enjoy the steak for ourselves alone. Therefore, for most of us, positive intentions and positive desires are not enough, because when we begin to manifest them as actions, our inherent nature of selfishness kicks in.

Abraham, however, had elevated himself to such a high spiritual level that when he thought, "I am giving up Isaac, I am willing to let him die, I'm willing to let him go," his thought was so pure, so complete, that it manifested as a completed action. Therefore, there was no need for Isaac to die physically. Whatever positive spiritual process Abraham had to undergo, the death of his son, Isaac, had already occurred in Abraham's mind.

There are many lessons we can learn from Abraham's thoughts and actions, and there is one in particular that I would like to mention. Abraham and Isaac were going to lose each other, but because Abraham was able to completely detach all ego and selfish desires from the relationship he had with his son, he got to keep Isaac not only in this physical world but forever.

The only way we can hold on to things that are true is if we are willing to completely detach all selfish attachments that we have for them. Abraham achieved this detachment completely in his mind. But for most of us, the ability to detach from all selfishness in a relationship is extremely difficult to achieve, so we have to use physical tools, or actions, to assist us.

The *Midrash* continues: Abraham had completed what the Creator desired of him in his mind prior to his actions. Abraham had already truly completed the sacrifice of Isaac in his mind. Therefore, the Creator said Abraham, "Do not do anything to Isaac. Now I see—not yesterday and not the day before, and not when I told you that you were going to have to give up Isaac—but at this moment, I see how pure you have perfected yourself, how you have completely detached yourself from all selfish attachments to Isaac. Do not do anything to Isaac. There is no need for anything physical to happen to Isaac."

Once Abraham had completed his thought of sacrificing Isaac as if it was action, there was no need for Isaac to be slaughtered. The *Midrash* says that the Creator told Abraham, "When I said to you, 'Take Isaac and bring him as a sacrifice,' at that time you had to bring him as a physical sacrifice. But at this moment, because of your complete pure thought, you don't have to give him up. Now, when I say to you, 'Do not do anything,' this is new. It is new and it is true now because you already did the work in your mind that would have been necessary to cause the physical pain prior to performing any action." This explanation from the Creator cleared up Abraham's confusion. What an enlightening process, and what an important lesson this is for all of us.

All of our attachments to physicality are going to end. All of our attachments to love of a selfish nature are going to end. Everything that has an element of selfishness, of *Desire to Receive for the Self Alone* in it, is going to die and that death is going to be painful. But there is a way to make sure this does not happen. On the Shabbat of Vayera we have the assistance of Abraham, who comes to our aid. It is impossible for any of us to accomplish our spiritual work without asking for the soul Abraham to help us!

The *Akedat Yitzhak* is a seminal moment of history that we constantly relive because the Light that Abraham revealed at the Binding of Isaac shines throughout all of history. The Light of this enormous sacrifice, which Abraham achieved in his mind, was a completed action that shines for us to this day.

When we truly understand this, and if we truly ask for the assistance of Abraham to help us, we can slowly but surely cut away all of our selfish attachments so that now nothing has to die. What is *Bila hamavet lanetzach*? What is "removal of death forever?" It is the moment when we, like Abraham, remove all of our selfish attachments and the Creator says there is no need for death anymore. Today, there is still a need for death in our world. We make death necessary because we are still attached to our *Desire to Receive for the Self Alone*. Because of our selfishness, the Creator says, "All the things that you love the most are going to have to die."

How do we get to the level of Abraham where the Creator will say, "Do not kill, do not allow death any more. There is no more need for death?" This is our spiritual work—the work Abraham began; the work we now have to complete. All those things and people we are attached to, all of our selfish ego connections—these are our Isaacs.

Unfortunately, the process of consciously removing our attachment to our "Isaac" is something we cannot do on our own. The Creator comes to us and says, "Listen, give it up. It is going to die, it is going to end, it is going to be painful." Now we have a choice: Do we allow the process to continue, for death to come, for pain to come, for love to end? Or do we do what Abraham did—a true *Akedat Yitzhak*? Do we, with the assistance of Abraham, do the work of giving up all attachments to physicality? Do we ask Abraham to give us the ability to kill off, to finish off all of our physical, selfish, *Desire to Receive for the Self Alone* attachments? When we choose to do this, then the death of death has to happen.

Bila hamavet lanetzach, the removal of death from this world, is not a gift that is given to us by the Creator. The Creator says,

"Right now, death is a gift for you. You cannot still go around with your selfishness, with your *Desire to Receive for the Self Alone*, because it is bad for you. Here, I will give you the gift of death—the pains of this world—to help you get rid of this selfishness." But we have another choice. There is the way of transformation, which is what Abraham chose. Abraham did the work. He completely gave up all attachments (that is, love of a selfish nature) to physicality, and then no death, no pain could occur.

The Ashes

What other lesson is there? This is such an enlightening, important, and crucial lesson. The *Talmud* says that the ashes from the burnt sacrifice of Isaac are always before the Creator. Just as we like to keep our favorite things close to us at all the times, so too, is the dust from the burning of the sacrifice of Isaac always before the Creator. What does this mean? We have just discussed how in the story of the Binding of Isaac, Isaac was *not* killed; therefore logically, there could be no cremated ashes of Isaac. Abraham's detachment was so complete that the sacrifice of Isaac totally manifested. Therefore, on a spiritual level these ashes do exist.

What are these ashes that are with the Creator all the time? These ashes are the wellspring from which we can draw the power to detach ourselves from all the things that cause us pain and, God forbid, death. These ashes from the altar are always before the Creator, because this is the one gift that we need to have constantly flowing to us.

ABRAHAM COMPLETED THE WORK

I would like to discuss one more related concept. The Bible says that as they walked to the sacrificial site, Abraham said to Isaac, "We will go to this place (*ko*)." The Hebrew word that Abraham used was *ko*, denoting something final. The Sfat Emet (Rabbi Yehuda Aryeh Leib Alter, 1847–1905) explains that when Abraham was walking with Isaac to the mountain, Abraham completely gave up and let go of Isaac to the point that he "killed" Isaac in his mind. Abraham knew that when he would kill Isaac there would be no more children to continue the work. Abraham knew that the only way his teachings and *bila hamavet laletzach* would be achieved in the world was through Isaac. The Creator had told Abraham that the continuation and thus, the perfection of our world would only come about through Isaac. Abraham, then, had a problem. How was the world going to achieve the *Gemar haTikkun* (Final Redemption) if Isaac was killed? Abraham knew that all the work of the perfection of humanity—all the Light that will ever be revealed—had to be accomplished while he walked with his son. Because Isaac was going to die, there could be no other time. Thus it was that Abraham completed the entire spiritual work of humanity for all times in a remarkably short time, and every year, on the Shabbat of Vayera, Abraham gives us all the energy of this gift. This gift of Abraham is something we need to truly appreciate.

Think about it! During Abraham's time with Isaac until the moment of the Binding, Abraham completed the entire work for all of humanity for all time. Abraham accomplished all the spiritual work for us through the strength and perfection of his thought alone. Do we have the strength today to achieve this same goal?

The Sfat Emet says that the Creator takes the thoughts of Abraham, which encompass all the perfection of humanity, and attaches them to our work. The *Midrash* goes even deeper to explain that the donkey that Abraham the Patriarch traveled on to perform the Binding of Isaac is the same donkey that Moses rode to take the children of Israel out of Egypt—and it is this same donkey that *Mashiach* will ride on at the Final Redemption. How do we know this to be true? Everything that we want to accomplish, Abraham already accomplished in the world of thought; the only action left for us to do is to manifest it. But we can only manifest it if we attach ourselves to the soul of Abraham.

Rav Ashlag mentions a beautiful section in the *Zohar*, one we need to remind ourselves of every day. The *Zohar* says that we cannot pray or do anything of a spiritual nature unless we attach ourselves to the souls of Abraham, Isaac, and Jacob, specifically of Abraham. Why? Because Abraham accomplished all the work that we could not possibly accomplish for ourselves. If we attach the thought of Abraham to whatever lowly actions we do, these actions can manifest in the *Gemar haTikkun*. What Abraham did then, he is waiting for us to manifest now.

The Shabbat of Vayera is an enlightening Shabbat on many levels, the most important of which is that it gives us the strength, from Abraham, to manifest *bila hamavet lanetzach* (the death of death). It gives us immortality.

Chayei Sarah

SARAH'S DESIRE TO BE AT THE GREAT REVELATION

In the story of Chayei Sarah, as is true with most of the stories in the *Book of Genesis*, there are many important lessons, some of which are almost beyond our comprehension. My goal with these teachings is to make sure that when we discuss these different ideas and concepts, we are then able to put this knowledge to work in our lives. However, I think it is important that we also learn and participate in teachings that are beyond us for two reasons: First, this gives us something to aspire to, and second, there is benefit in stretching our consciousness, even when these new concepts are not ideas that we can fully comprehend.

In *The Gift of the Bible*, Rav Ashlag tells us that when an individual strengthens and awakens his consciousness in his spiritual work, this awakening influences the rest of the world.

This is a concept that we have heard many times, and it is one that we need to focus on. We should be aware that when we comprehend a spiritual lesson that influences our own consciousness, this comprehension in turn influences the rest of the world. Therefore, not only do we have a responsibility to change the way we act, but we have an even greater responsibility to transform the way we think—to transform our consciousness.

We should be constantly asking ourselves: "Is my consciousness any different now than it was a month ago or six months ago? Is it stronger, is it expanding, is it greater?" It is important not only to look at our actions, but also to make sure that there is progress in our consciousness. Without such progress we will never be able to achieve the ultimate purpose for which we came to this world: We will never be able to truly influence the consciousness of the world to the degree that is our destiny.

I would like to share a beautiful teaching in the *Midrash* concerning the death of Sarah. The biblical chapter known as Chayei Sarah speaks about the death and burial of Sarah, and about the uniting of Isaac and Rebecca.

Sarah was unique among the matriarchs. The *Zohar* cites many reasons why Sarah is the only matriarch whose death, funeral, and burial place spark such lengthy discussion in the Bible. In the previous Bible chapter of Vayera, we learned about the Binding of Isaac, where God came to Abraham and said, "Go and bring your son, Isaac, as a sacrifice." The *Midrash* tells us that Abraham did not tell Sarah what he was going to do, but the Satan came to Sarah and asked, "Do you know what is about to happen right now?" And Sarah replied, "What is about to happen?" The Satan then said, "Your husband, Abraham, is taking your only son, Isaac, and he is going to sacrifice him. He is going to kill him." The *Midrash* says that at that moment, Sarah was so terrified that Abraham was going to kill her son, Isaac, that she had a heart attack and died.

But this does not make much sense. We know that someone on Sarah's spiritual level would not become so overwhelmingly terrified by this news. Terrible as the news was, Sarah would have understood that something beyond the physical event was taking place. In much the same way, we too, must take into account that the way this story is told in the *Midrash* is not something we can accept in a literal way.

Whenever I read about the conversation between Sarah and the Satan, the first thought that crosses my mind—and an important concept for all of us to keep in mind—is that Sarah was not a simple person. The great Kabbalist, the *Ohev Yisrael* (Rabbi Avraham Yehoshua Heshil, 1748–1825, also known as the Apta Rebbe), tells us that Sarah understood the depth of the awesome Light that would be revealed at the Binding of Isaac (*Akedat Yitzchak*). She knew Isaac was not going to die. In fact, she knew not only that Isaac was never meant to die, but that a tremendous revelation of Light was about to occur at Mount Moriah, the place where the Temple would eventually be built.

WHAT GOD MEANT
❧ Chayei Sarah ❧

We cannot truly even begin to fathom the amount of Light that was revealed at the *Akedat Yitzchak*. Sarah knew that the Binding of Isaac was going to be one of the pinnacles of human existence—one of the pinnacles of revelation of Light in our world—so much so that now, thousands of years later, when we come to the important cosmic times of *Rosh Hashanah* and *Yom Kippur*, we re-awaken this Light of the *Akedat Yitzchak* and we request of the Creator that this Light continue to shine down to us, to create a positive year for us.

When Sarah heard that this awesome revelation of Light was to occur at the Temple Mount, she desired to be a part of it. Sarah wanted to partake of and be part of that great revelation of Light. But Sarah had a problem: The Binding was to take place imminently, and if she walked, even if she rode on a donkey to get there, she would not reach Mount Moriah in time. So Sarah made a very simple decision. She said, "I can stay in this physical world a little bit longer, but that could not possibly compare to being present at the *Akedah*, to participate in that great revelation of Light."

Then and there, Sarah made the conscious decision to leave this physical world so that her soul, in its complete form, could go to Mount Moriah where the *Akedah* was taking place. This is why Sarah left this world. She left this world because she decided to participate in the awesome revelation of Light about to take place. Sarah did not want to continue to live in her physical body if it was going to hold her back from connecting to this great Light. So her soul left her body and she went to the *Akedah*, where she partook of this great revelation of Light.

This is why the Bible says that Sarah died in Kiryat Arba (literally: Town of the Four). The Bible says Sarah died with a complete connection to the Name of God—the Tetragrammaton (*Yud, Hei, Vav,* and *Hei*) and *Adonai* (*Alef, Dalet, Nun,* and *Yud*). Sarah achieved this complete connection because, even while she was still alive, she had no connection to the *Desire to Receive for the Self Alone.* The explanation in the *Midrash* was not that Sarah got scared and had a heart attack, but rather that she made a conscious decision to be present on Mount Moriah at the Binding of Isaac and to partake of this great revelation of Light.

What an enlightening and beautiful lesson! Sarah knew that she could reveal more Light for the world if she went out from her body, and so she did. For her, it was a simple decision.

Rav Ashlag faced a comparable moment in his life with equal decisiveness. He and his wife lived in Warsaw at a time when travel to Israel was difficult, and life there was often arduous and uncertain. One day, Rav Ashlag said to his wife, "I know that I have finished my personal job in this world, my personal transformation, and now I have two options. I can either leave this physical body because I have no more work to do with it, or I can go to Israel and reveal Light for the world." When his wife heard this, she realized there was no discussion. So she agreed that they should go to live in Israel.

How many of us constantly strive to make our spiritual work about our connection to the Light of the Creator—the revelation of Light in the world—so we can bring an end to pain and suffering? This consciousness is not easily achieved, but it certainly is a consciousness that we should awaken within ourselves. We should constantly be asking, "How far away am I from the true consciousness that my entire life is truly about revealing this Light in the world?" And we can set as a goal for ourselves—emulating the mindset of Sarah, or Rav Ashlag—that our work of revealing Light will continue, whether it takes place in our physical body or not.

When we read about the death of Sarah, we reveal and connect, to one degree or another, to this great revelation of Light that Sarah achieved at Kiryat Arba. Sarah achieved a complete connection to the Light of the Creator, to the Name of God— the Tetragrammaton and the *Alef, Dalet, Nun,* and *Yud*— because she acted upon her desire to completely give up her *Desire to Receive for the Self Alone*—her body consciousness, to be at Mount Moriah for that awesome revelation of Light.

SHARING AS A SERVANT

The second lesson I would like to discuss concerns Eliezer, servant of Abraham and the closest person to him. Eliezer is known as *Eliezer eved Avraham* (Eliezer, the servant of Abraham). As the *Midrash* explains, his name was actually *Dammeseq Eliezer*, literally meaning Eliezer from Damascus, and he was the student who was closest to Abraham. Not only was Eliezer able to understand the wisdom of Abraham, he was also capable of conveying this wisdom to other people. Many students throughout history have had the ability to comprehend the wisdom of their teacher and to pass this wisdom on to others—Rav Chaim Vital with Rav Isaac Luria, and Rav Abba with Rabbi Shimon bar Yochai, just to name two—but in this case, we are talking about comprehending the wisdom of a teacher on the level of Abraham, whose wisdom was far beyond what we can imagine, and then also having the ability to give that wisdom over to others. This is a tremendous spiritual level of achievement.

Before his death, Rav Isaac Luria (the Ari) made all his students promise that they would not teach anyone what they had learned from him. The Ari knew that even though there were many great souls amongst his students, none of them completely comprehended his wisdom, and therefore, none of them was capable of teaching it to others.

With the example of the Ari in mind, we can hardly even start to imagine the level of consciousness and connection to the Light of the Creator that Dammeseq Eliezer must have possessed.

The Bible says Eliezer traveled to the city of Nahor, where Rebecca lived, and asked the Creator to give him a sign to identify who the future wife of Isaac would be. The Torah is meticulous in its use of language; there are no extra or insignificant words. Very often, tremendous lessons can be learned from one letter or from a single word. The *Midrash* asks why the Torah spends so much time first telling us the story of Eliezer and his meeting with

Rebecca and then repeating the story when Eliezer recounts it in detail to Rebecca's family. Why does the Torah devote so many words to this story when we know how particular and specific the Torah is about the use of extra words?

To answer this question, the *Midrash* uses an interesting phrase; it says, "*gedola* (greater) are the words of the stories of the servants of the patriarchs (here, Abraham) than is the study of their children," meaning that there is something so unique and powerful about the stories of the servants of the patriarchs, as told in the Bible, that these stories are greater than all the studying that comes afterward.

To understand this, we need to go back to Eliezer. The Bible says that when Eliezer came to Nahor to find a wife for Abraham's son, Isaac, he came with a tremendous amount of wealth—animals and gold and jewelry. However, when Eliezer introduced himself to Rebecca and to her family, he said, "*Eved Avraham anochi*" (I am the servant of Abraham). There are many ways that Eliezer could have introduced himself. Had he introduced himself as Abraham's closest friend, or his closest student, or his most trusted confidant, all these descriptions would have been equally true.

Out of all the possible ways Eliezer could have introduced himself, he chose to say, "*Eved Avraham anochi*" (I am a servant of Abraham), indicating to us that within the word "servant," there is a tremendous secret. Abraham did not ask Eliezer to call himself "Abraham's servant." I'm sure if it had been Abraham's decision, he would have said, "Tell them that you are my best student, you are my closest friend, and my most trustworthy confidant." But Eliezer said, "No, for me, it is important that I am known as *eved Avraham* (the servant of Abraham)."

As mentioned previously, the entire purpose of our life is to transform our *Desire to Receive* to the *Desire to Share*. There are many different ways one can share, but for the purposes of this teaching, I would like to mention just two of them. The first level of sharing is where we—in one way or another, whether consciously or unconsciously, whether in words or in actions— do a favor for another person. We have all shared in this way at one time or another.

But among the very highest is a level of sharing known as "servant" (*eved*). When the Torah describes the greatest heights that Moses achieved spiritually, the words used are: *"Moshe Avdi"* (Moses, My servant). This higher level of sharing as "servant" is something completely unique. When we no longer feel that we have the ability to say "no," when we no longer feel that we have a choice whether to give or not to give, our consciousness becomes one of a servant. We become a servant, not in the sense of being lower in the social pecking order, but in the sense of how we give and how we share. This consciousness may be higher than where most of us are today, but it is certainly not higher than we can comprehend.

We can all attain this level of sharing, but before we understand how we can achieve this on a practical level, it is important to differentiate between the level of being a servant in sharing and being a victim in sharing. We can see this distinction when it comes to giving, for example.

There are many people who *give*, whether to their children, their spouse, or their friends; the reason they give is because they would feel uncomfortable if they said no. These people are practically enslaved by this type of giving. They do not truly want to give, but they give anyway, later becoming upset and frazzled by their decision. This type of giving is what I would describe as being a victim in giving. When it came to sharing, neither Moses nor Eliezer shared because they were *victims* of sharing. On the contrary, they shared as *servants* because there was no reason to be a servant, yet they made a conscious decision to be one. Such situations, the Torah makes clear, are the greatest seeds for true growth, for true connection.

I recently planned to share some time with someone, which I was looking forward to because such meetings give me an opportunity to socialize and possibly teach something at the same time. But on the day that we were scheduled to meet, I did not feel well. I was about to postpone the meeting and move it forward a couple of days when I remembered the concept of being a servant in sharing. I thought, "If I am truly a servant to the person I am supposed to meet, if I want to grow this consciousness within me, I cannot postpone the meeting. Yes, it would be easier for me to meet at a later date, but if I am a servant, I do not have a choice. I must do it on the appointed day." This is the level of consciousness we are discussing here.

This is not being a victim of sharing. We are speaking about quite the opposite—when we have a strong desire not simply to share, but to awaken within ourselves the consciousness of being a servant. Most of us share, but how many of us share with the consciousness of being a servant? I think if we are truly honest with ourselves, our answer is almost never.

The story of Eliezer meeting Rebecca is repeated twice in the Bible because the Creator knew we would not comprehend the spiritual message the first time, so the Creator allowed Eliezer to repeat it a second time. *Eved Avraham anochi* was the consciousness in every word that Eliezer said and in every action he performed. The constant message was: "I am not Abraham's friend; I am not his confidant; I am not his right-hand man. I am his servant."

Eliezer knew that by awakening this awareness and desire—the consciousness of being a servant in sharing—the highest levels in our world can be achieved. Therefore, as we discuss this concept together, we awaken within ourselves the desire and awareness of being a servant of sharing. None of us will attain this level today or tomorrow, but by awakening a desire for this consciousness, we are taking an all-important first step.

The *Midrash* says that greater than all the study of the Torah is the *ma'aseh avot* (being a servant of sharing), and it illustrates this point with the story of Eliezer showing his servitude in sharing when he did not have to. Again, Eliezer could have introduced himself as the right-hand man of one of the wealthiest and most connected people in the world, but he knew that the path to true connection was to awaken sharing in the way of being a servant. Now that we are aware that to truly connect to the Light of the Creator means we have to awaken our sharing in the way of being a servant, it is important to understand that this is not going to be easy, nor is it going to be comfortable. But we should do it once, then do it twice a week, and then do it three times a week, and so on, always remembering that if we truly want to connect to the Light of the Creator, being a servant of sharing is the pathway.

RIDICULOUS SHARING

The third idea I would like to raise concerns Eliezer's arrival at the well when he said to the Creator, "Please give me a sign. When I ask for something to drink, whichever girl replies, 'I will give you to drink and I will give all of your camels and everyone who has accompanied you to drink,' I will know this is the one who should be the wife of Isaac."

There is much discussion about the nature of this unusual request. We know from previous verses in this story that Eliezer was exceptionally strong physically; in fact, the Bible says: "almost stronger than a few hundred men." Eliezer said that he would arrive at the well with a caravan of people and animals, and find a girl (whom we can assume would not be as strong as he was) and say to her, "Give me something to drink." This girl would then reply, "I will give you to drink, I will give all the people with you to drink," meaning she would do the physical work of putting the bucket down into the well and bringing it back up, time and time again, until everyone of Eliezer's caravan was satiated.

How many of us would look at this girl and think she was a high soul? I think most of us would think she was crazy because there is absolutely no logic in this sequence of events. Think about it. If we were standing by a well and a huge brute came toward us with a large group of people and camels following behind him and said, "Could you give us something to drink," would any of us even think for a moment that we should help him? It seems ridiculous. First, this person appears to be so much stronger than we are, so why doesn't he get the water himself? And second, it seems crazy to volunteer to give water to all the people with him as well.

Furthermore, it says in the *Midrash* that as Eliezer came to the well, a miracle occurred for Rebecca. The water from the well rose toward her so that she would not have to lower the bucket all the way down to the bottom of the well.

If we were looking for a wife for our son or for somebody else's son and we saw a physical miracle occurring for this girl, would that not be sign enough? None of us has ever probably seen water rising to the top of the well in a miraculous way, the way it did for Rebecca. Why is Eliezer now testing God by saying, "It is wonderful to see that this girl is so connected to You that she can do miracles whenever she wants, but I still want to make sure." It doesn't make any sense. Rebecca was obviously a tremendous soul if she was able to perform this miracle with the well, so why should further proof be needed?

There are two very important lessons we can learn here. First, Eliezer wanted to make sure that this girl, this potential wife for Isaac, was not going to be someone who was sufficiently connected to the Light only for this one miracle to occur, but that she was someone who was going to continuously grow in her connection to the Light of the Creator. The fact that someone can perform a miracle today does not mean that they are going to be growing spiritually in their connection to the Light of the Creator ten years from now. The miracle means only that this individual is connected today. This is an important lesson for us.

The only way for Eliezer to know whether Rebecca would continue to grow was if she was willing to be ridiculous in her sharing. For us, too, the only way to be certain that we are going to grow is if we reach a point where we realize that nothing that we do in our lives, none of the connections that we will make in our lives, can bring us to the point of continuous growth and connection to the Light of the Creator unless we are constantly and consistently sharing ridiculously—or to use the term mentioned previously: sharing as a servant.

When Rebecca was given the opportunity to share with Eliezer, she realized that the only way that she could grow in her connection, thereby achieving fulfillment in her life, was if she constantly pushed herself to share ridiculously. The only way to know whether we are going to grow from now to next year is by how much ridiculous sharing we do.

Even if we were able to create this type of miracle—most of us probably cannot, but even if we could—this in and of itself would not be enough. There are many other actions we can perform that will give us a connection today and tomorrow, but the only true test of our continual growth is how much ridiculous sharing we do each day. Let us ask ourselves the question: "How much ridiculous sharing have I done in this past week, in this past month?" If we were to answer this question truthfully, we would probably say, "Very little."

What we understand from Rebecca and Eliezer is that the only way to guarantee our constant growth and connection to the Light of the Creator—and thus our fulfillment and happiness—is by consistently practicing ridiculous sharing. The question we have to ask ourselves honestly and truthfully should not simply be: "Am I sharing, or connecting?" It should be: "Am I sharing ridiculously?" Only if this becomes a main focus of our lives are we guaranteed—as Eliezer was guaranteed with Rebecca—that there will be a constant growth, a constant connection, ultimately leading to the level of perfection Rebecca achieved.

"Am I sharing ridiculously?" This was the one question Eliezer needed answered, and this is the single question we have to ask ourselves if we are to achieve the ultimate purpose of our lives.

THE DANGER OF NEEDING APPROVAL

When we study from kabbalistic teachings and the insights of the sages, it is enlightening to realize how wrong we can sometimes be in our initial understanding of the Bible stories. With that in mind, the reason I am passionate about the story of Toldot is because of the many secrets contained within the relationship between Jacob and Esau.

Esau is portrayed as the bad guy, and Jacob the good guy—this is very clear, black and white. However, the Bible says: "Isaac loved Esau," which does not make any sense if Esau was who most of us think he was. Clearly, the Bible is showing us that we need to change our perception of Esau.

The lineage of Jacob began with his grandfather, Abraham, and followed with his father, Isaac. For most of his life, Jacob knew that his father did not love him as much as he loved Esau. Can you imagine the amount of pain this must have caused Jacob throughout his entire life? Jacob knew his brother Esau was an evil person, or at least not as pure and as elevated as he was, yet their father, Isaac—one of the greatest souls to ever live in our world, loved Esau more than he loved Jacob. On the surface, there was Abraham, Isaac, and Jacob—one happy family. But it was not like that. There is a lot to be learned here, but first, I would like to explore the greatness, the righteousness of Esau.

The Mei HaShiloach (Rav Mordechai Joseph Leiner, 1801 –1854) teaches that the Midrash says that when Esau spoke with Isaac, he would speak about lofty matters and details of his spiritual work. This made Esau not only sound like an extremely spiritual person, but also made him appear to be one of the most caring and elevated spiritual people of that time.

The *Midrash* explains that Isaac loved Esau because Esau had the ability to win Isaac over with his mouth.

When people read this *Midrash*, they probably think Esau was just a liar—that he wanted his father to think that he was a good guy—and that the self-portrait he was painting for Isaac, in his conversations with his father, was exactly the opposite of who he truly was. It is understandable that someone would think Esau was a truly negative person and that he used conversations with Isaac to make it appear as if he was interested in spiritual matters and focused on his spiritual work. However, this was not the case. Even if Esau had truly been as evil and cunning a liar as it would appear from the *Midrash*, Isaac would not have been fooled.

Initially, Jacob and Esau were equal in their purity, in their spiritual connection, in their study, in their elevation. What was Esau's downfall? Only one thing: Esau wanted his father to approve of him.

Jacob and Esau started out in the same place: They had great parents and both were elevated in their spiritual work. There was only one difference: How Isaac viewed him was important to Esau. It was important to Esau that his father knew how spiritual he was. This is was what finished Esau off and led him to fall.

Can you imagine this? Jacob and Esau began from the same place. They were both elevated, they both studied, they both did their spiritual work. But because it was important to Esau that his father knew what he was doing—that Isaac knew how elevated he was in his spiritual work—Esau engineered his own downfall.

Why did Esau want his father to love him? It was not because of the silly ego-desire that most of us have—that we want people to think that we are good people. The only reason Esau wanted his father to love him was so Isaac would pray for him. Esau said to Isaac, "Look, Dad, I am working hard, I am studying, I am not sleeping at night. Please pray to God that I gain more wisdom, that I am able to be spiritual." This is what destroyed Esau.

By contrast, Jacob's attitude was simple: "I don't care if my father, Isaac, thinks I am great, or if he thinks I am terrible, or if he prays for me, or if he does not. If I am doing what the

Creator wants me to do, then the Creator will make sure that my father prays for me."

Jacob and Esau, these two tremendous souls, who were purer and more elevated than any of us can ever hope to be, would sit and study together. When Esau would say to Jacob, "Jacob, let us talk to our father; after all, the whole world comes to him for prayers and for blessings. Let us talk to him and show him how hard we are working so that he can pray for us."

Jacob would not agree. Instead, he would reply, "No, Esau, we have to just do the work. Who cares what anyone else—even our father—knows? Just do the work."

The Mei Hashiloach continues, "Because Jacob separated himself from any need for his work to be acknowledged by his father, he put his certainty in the Creator. He understood if he did the right thing, the Creator would make sure that the right thing would come to him. Whoever does not have complete certainty in the Creator and puts himself in this place of Esau (where Esau went to his father and said, "Look at what I am doing; give me the assistance"), God forbid, will wind up like Esau."

The power of this revelation changes our perception. We should all leave this discussion with a new love for Esau, who was a remarkable individual, beyond anything we can imagine for ourselves. Esau's singular downfall was his need, not for approval, but for Isaac to pray for him, for his spiritual work to go beyond the Creator. Our spiritual work needs to be only between us and the Creator. We should fight to make sure it does not go beyond that. Not even for the best reasons in the world—and there is no purer reason than having your father pray for you.

If you had the opportunity for Isaac to pray for you, to help you in your spiritual work, would you not want to go and talk to him about it? No, we cannot risk sharing our spiritual work, even with Isaac, if our motive is recognition.

We have to know that, God forbid, if we have any desire for people to see what we are doing, for people to know what we are doing, that this desire can finish us off spiritually, as it did Esau. We must fight to make sure no one knows about anything we do, whether it is what we study, what work we do, anything. If anyone knows, they should know as little as possible.

Unfortunately, many of us have the opposite consciousness. If we do not get credit, if people do not know what we have done, if people do not give us recognition for the great work that we do, it depresses us, it upsets us. We need to understand that this desire for recognition is the kiss of death; it will finish us off spiritually, as it did Esau. Our spiritual work has to be only between us and the Creator. It is too dangerous for us to allow anyone to find out about our spiritual work.

However, we do have teachers with whom we can share, and there is a need for that. What I am discussing here is all the rest of the nonsense that goes on—all the rest of the stuff where we feel the need to be recognized, and to know, and to let know. But as we learn from Esau, this kills our spiritual work. What an astonishing lesson!

BLESSINGS COME FROM SITUATIONS THAT SEEM UNFAIR AND WRONG

Many of the commentators, the *Zohar* included, struggle with Isaac's desire to give the blessings to Esau because it is known that the day of the blessing would set in motion the world's future process—a path of Light or a path of darkness.

The *Zohar* asks: "How did Isaac not know the truth about Esau? Isaac had the Shechinah (the Light of the Creator) and *Ruach HaKodesh* (Divine Inspiration) with him all the time. But although the *Shechinah* was constantly with Isaac, It did not let him know the truth. The *Shechinah* allowed Isaac to live most of his life with a false understanding of Esau, in order for the blessings to come to Jacob concealed from Isaac's understanding, beyond Isaac's consciousness, and only in the Thought of the Creator. The blessings had to be given in this way to ensure a path of Light. It was only when the Light of the Creator accompanied Jacob as he entered Isaac's tent that Isaac realized the blessings needed to come directly from the Creator."

What the *Zohar* is explaining here is that these blessings could not come from Isaac; they had to come only from the Creator. Isaac was the conduit, but he could not give the blessings consciously, because if he had done so, he would have diminished the power of the blessings. The blessings had to be given in such a way that his consciousness was not involved and therefore, could not diminish the blessings.

Although there are many lessons to learn here, we now have a better understanding from the Mei HaShiloach that Jacob did not truly experience much pain because Isaac favored Esau. The *Zohar* says it had to be this way, because when the blessings were to come, God had to make sure that Isaac did not give them to Jacob with his own consciousness, with his own desire. For over sixty years, Jacob had to be in this place of darkness so that when the blessings came, they would come in the correct way.

If the beginning of Jacob's life had been ideal—where his father loved him and knew everything he was doing—that would have been well and good, but when it came time for Isaac to give the blessings to Jacob, the world would have lost out because, God forbid, Isaac's blessings would have been diminished by his consciousness.

When Isaac gave his blessings to Jacob, he gave Jacob all the strength and all the ability to bring about the *Gemar HaTikkun* (Final Redemption). If Jacob would have had an easy life, one where Isaac knew who he was and desired to give him the blessings, the world would have lost great Light. We would not ever be able to achieve the *Gemar HaTikkun*.

Many times, we find ourselves in situations where we do not understand why we are treated in a certain way. It is obvious we should be treated in some other way, that the situation should be different than what it is. The lesson for us is that when blessings are to due come down to us, these blessings need to come from a place beyond our understanding. The situation when this happens is going to appear to be mistaken and amiss, with everyone treating us in the wrong way. But this is when the real blessings come—when everything appears wrong. In the case of Jacob, for the blessings to come from the Creator and not from Isaac, Jacob had to have a difficult time with his father for most of his life. Even after Jacob received the blessings, he ran away from Esau and Isaac did not see him.

When we are in situations that appear mistaken on the surface, we should remember that great blessings, real blessings, can only become manifest this one way—where the blessings come purely from the Creator and not diminished by being filtered through anyone.

If we want the blessings that come into our lives to be of a pure, complete form, we have to be willing to accept them *le mala lo lada'at* (without our understanding). In other words, we have to be willing to accept situations that appear incorrect. This is a very important lesson that we can manifest in both great and small ways.

DRAWING BLESSINGS BY FEELING THE PAIN OF THE WORLD

Jacob was simple, but his simplicity was a problem. For the Light of the Creator to be revealed on the day of the blessings, there needed to be a Vessel. When there is no Vessel, Light cannot be revealed.

The commentators explain that in the history of humankind, the day of the blessings by Isaac was unique because the Gates of Heaven were open to reveal the entirety of the Light of Redemption to our world. Isaac knew that this great Light of Redemption needed to be brought down into our world, but there was a problem. Jacob in his simplicity had not created the Vessel within himself to contain this Light; he had not awakened his desire, which was this Vessel for the Light.

Jacob did not have the desire, so Isaac could not give the blessings to him. Isaac knew Esau was not the right person to give the blessings to, but he thought it best to still give the blessing to Esau and reveal the Light in the world, rather than leaving the Light in the Endless World where it could not be touched, so that when Jacob became awakened, he would have a place from where to draw the Light.

The revelation of Light in this world is a three-step process. First, there is Light in the Endless World, which most of us cannot touch. Second, we have teachers and conduits—middle level—who draw down this Light and prepare the reservoir. Third, when the student (the Vessel) is ready to receive the Light, he or she can then manifest the Light to whatever degree he or she is ready to receive it.

The Ari with his student, Rav Chaim Vital, and Rav Ashlag's teacher with Rav Ashlag, were conduits to draw this great Light down and give it to the Vessels of their students. Isaac was the conduit to draw the Light of Redemption for Jacob (his son and Vessel) and give it to him.

What did Rebecca do when she overheard Isaac tell Esau to prepare him food so that he could bless him? Rebecca took Esau's clothing (the Vessel of Esau) and dressed Jacob in it. Esau's clothing is a metaphor here for the pain of *Galut Edom* (the Exile of Edom), which we still experience today. By dressing Jacob in Esau's clothing, Rebecca awakened Jacob's desire for the Light and she said, "Jacob, you cannot live simply anymore. You have to awaken a greater Vessel. Put on the clothing of Esau (meaning, take on the pain that is in the world) to awaken this greater Vessel."

Rebecca explained to Jacob, "Now is not the time for simplicity. On this day, there is to be a great revelation of the Light of the *Gemar HaTikkun* (Final Redemption). But you do not have the Vessel to receive the Light. You cannot receive it because you do not feel or experience the pain that is in the world. Take upon yourself the clothing of Esau. Take upon yourself the darkness called *Galut Edom* (Exile of Edom)." Jacob needed his mother's assistance to awaken within him the understanding and desire to create this Vessel to receive the Light. When Jacob came to Isaac in the tent, Isaac asked him, "Do you have the Vessel (meaning, do you feel the pain that is within the world)? If you do not feel the pain, Jacob, if you do not have the clothing of Esau surrounding you, if you do not feel this weight upon you, you do not have the Vessel for the Light of the *Gemar HaTikkun*." But Jacob now had the Vessel of Esau; he had awakened it by taking the pain of the world upon himself.

Rebecca told Jacob then—and is telling us now—that to the degree we take upon ourselves this weight, the pain that is within our world, will we have the Vessel to receive the blessings from Isaac. Jacob had to put on the clothing of Esau, and Isaac needed to feel that clothing before he was able to give Jacob the immense blessings of the Light of the *Gemar HaTikkun*. This story teaches us that you and I are destined to reveal much more Light of the *Gemar HaTikkun* (Final Redemption) than we currently manifest in our world today, and what we are missing is the clothing of Esau—that awakening in ourselves of the pain that is within the world.

To understand that every one of us, to one degree or another is like Jacob is one of the immense gifts of the Shabbat of Toldot. There is a tremendous amount of Light and blessings that we are meant to reveal, but we are not revealing them today. The reason why we are not revealing this Light and these blessings is our lack of acceptance, our unwillingness to take upon ourselves the clothing of Esau, the pain that is within this world.

On the Shabbat of Toldot, we can come to Isaac for blessings. On this Shabbat, Isaac is here to give us these blessings: The blessings of the ability to bring the Finale Redemption. But Isaac is telling us, "On this Shabbat, you cannot receive the blessings from me until I have seen and felt that you have taken upon yourself the pain that is within this world. Without this consciousness, you do not have a Vessel, and without a Vessel, I cannot give you the blessings."

Rav Ashlag explains, that the Shabbat of Toldot offers us the opportunity to once more reveal the great blessings and power to achieve the *Gemar HaTikkun*. But we can only receive this tremendous infusion of Light once we have truly taken upon ourselves the pain within the world. Only to the degree that we dress ourselves in the pain of this world, in the pain of this exile, can Isaac give us the blessings of the *Gemar HaTikkun* on this Shabbat. Rav Ashlag makes it very clear: This is the work we have to do in order to receive these blessings from Isaac.

JACOB HELPS THE ANGELS

Each story of the Bible has many inner secrets and teachings to reveal, and the story of Vayetze is no exception.

The Bible says Jacob left Beer Sheva, where he lived with his parents, and traveled to Charan. Jacob arrived at Beit El (later I will explain what this means). It is here that he slept and dreamt his famous dream of angels ascending and descending a ladder. Rabbi Yonatan ben Uziel, the Amukah, asks, "Who are these angels?" The *Zohar* and the *Midrash* have many explanations concerning the angels, but the Amukah explains something very intriguing—that when Jacob left his father Isaac's house, angels came to accompany him.

Who were those angels accompanying Jacob? The answer is found in the story of the destruction of the cities of Sodom and Gomorrah. Before the Creator destroyed the two cities, He

103

sent three angels to Abraham to warn him of the impending destruction. Then these same angels went to the two cities themselves. When two of the angels came to Sodom, they told all its inhabitants that they had come to the city to destroy it. Because angels are not supposed to reveal the heavenly secrets, these two were banished from their seats around the Creator.

For this reason, these two angels were not in service of the Creator. However, when the time came for Jacob to leave his home in Beer Sheva, they were given an opportunity to redeem themselves by protecting Jacob, which they did as they walked with him in mercy until he reached the city of Beit El. Once the angels had safely escorted Jacob as far as Beit El, they were granted permission to re-enter Heaven. On entering Heaven, they spoke to all the other angels and said, "Remember us? We were banished and have not been with you for a long time. Now the Creator has granted us permission to return. Come with us and see the beauty of the countenance of Jacob. Remember how at the creation of the world, all the faces, all the countenances of the righteous people would come and sit at the *Kisei HaKavod* (Chair of Honor)." The *Kisei HaKavod*, by the way, does not refer to a physical chair; it is a spiritual level.

The angels continued, "You remember this face, this Light of Jacob, which we were all excited would one day come down to this world? Well, it is here now. We were with him. Come down and see." These two angels took the group of angels to the ladder between Heaven and Earth and showed them how to descend the ladder to view the countenance of Jacob. The angels ascending the ladder were the two angels who had been granted permission to re-enter heaven. The descending angels were the angels that desired to look upon the countenance of Jacob, to see his face.

This is a pleasant story. But the question is why were those two angels who were kicked out of Heaven for revealing the Creator's secrets regarding Sodom and Gomorrah sent to protect Jacob. They were sent to protect Jacob so that they could complete their *tikkun* (correction) through this process.

The *Zohar* tells us that the Creator will not perform an action without first informing either the prophets or the righteous people. This is the power of a *tzadik* (a righteous person). Righteous people have the gift of prophecy: They can see, God forbid, darkness or judgment that is meant to come to this world. The purpose of this prophecy is to create the opportunity for change. My thought is that possibly these angels, although they had overstepped their authority in Sodom and Gomorrah, helped to open up this channel of the righteous foreseeing the future for the purpose of altering it.

The *Midrash* explains that the story of Vayetze is the beginning of the *Galut*, the Exile—the time of entering into darkness. The spiritual correction of these two angels involved their coming to Jacob and saying, "We have opened up a channel for you—and for all the righteous souls that follow you—to see all the darkness that is meant to come to this world so that you can change it." Thus, their correction was through Jacob.

ONCE YOU MAKE THE COMMITMENT,
MIRACLES WILL HAPPEN

It is important to remind ourselves that when we look a little deeper into the literal meaning of a story in the Torah (Bible) we realize that it is not at all as it appears to be. Jacob left Beer Sheva and traveled north to Charan. If we map this out, we see that Beer Sheva is almost in the geographic center of present-day Israel, while Charan is all the way up north, in southeastern Turkey.

During his travels, Jacob arrived at Beit El where he spent the night. However, there is much confusion regarding Jacob's journey to Beit El. In the *Midrash*, Rabbi Elazar, quoting Rabbi Yosi ben Zimra, said, "This ladder that Jacob saw in his dream had its feet in Beer Sheva, the city in which Isaac and Jacob lived, and from where Jacob left. The middle of the ladder was in Jerusalem, above Mount Moriah, and Beit El to the north of Jerusalem. Charan, the city Jacob desired to travel to, was at the topmost end of the ladder, above Beit El."

The *Midrash* asks: "Why did the Creator reveal Himself to Jacob at Beit El as opposed to in the city of Jerusalem, where the Light of the Creator rested at Mount Moriah, the place of the Holy Temple?" Let us go through the geography once more so we are clear. Beer Sheva is in the south, Jerusalem is the middle point, and Beit El is above Jerusalem and closer to Charan, which is in the north. Jacob traveled from Beer Sheva to his destination, Charan. He passed through Jerusalem and

Beit El and then finally reached Charan. Jacob then decided to travel back to Jerusalem. On the way, he became tired and lay down to sleep in Beit El, and it was then that the Creator said, "Jacob is coming through My House; let Me ask him to stay the night."

The *Midrash* says that what actually happened was that the part of Jerusalem on which the Holy Temple stands literally detached from the ground and traveled to Beit El to be with Jacob. The most important plot of land in the world traveled all the way to Beit El to be with Jacob!

But Jacob had arrived at the Creator's House earlier in his journey, so why would the Creator now bring His House to Beit El (literally, House of God) to where Jacob was now? Why did the Creator not stop Jacob in Jerusalem at Mount Moriah during Jacob's journey north and say, "Jacob, I know you have a long trek ahead of you to reach Charan. Why not stay here the night?"

The Creator answers this question when He says, "If Jacob could not awaken himself to pray at Mount Moriah, where the Binding of Isaac took place and a location that both his ancestors, Abraham and Isaac, knew was a tremendously powerful and important spiritual site, I am not going to tell him to stop and pray."

First, the Creator appeared to be angry with Jacob. "How dare you not stop and pray in Jerusalem on your way?" Then, after Jacob decided to go all the way back to Jerusalem to pray, the

Creator created this unbelievable miracle for him. The Creator brought Jerusalem all the way up to Beit El. If the Creator was angry with Jacob, why did the Creator not let him walk all the way back to Jerusalem? How come the Creator brought Jerusalem all the way to Beit El? Why create a miracle for someone whom you believe has failed?

We learn a tremendous and inspiring lesson here. Once a person decides to do the right thing, once a person decides that he or she wants to do everything in their power to connect to the Light of the Creator, miracles will occur to support them. If a person does not have the desire, if a person does not have full commitment, nothing will happen. Although Jacob initially traveled through Jerusalem without stopping, he still received this enormous blessing and miracle of the angels and the ladder. To receive the gift of the ability to end the *Galut*, to end the exile, is a momentous occurrence in human history.

While Jacob traveled to Charan, he was worried that his brother might try to kill him. Jacob also worried about spiritual matters, but while he traveled through Jerusalem, he did not awaken himself to pray there. Can you imagine what would have happened if Jacob had not finally awakened himself once he reached Charan? This unbelievable gift of ending pain, suffering, and death in our world was waiting in Jerusalem, and Jacob passed right through the city. What was the Creator thinking at that moment? "Oh, this is the end!"

When Jacob left Beer Sheva, the Creator informed all the angels that Jacob was their man. Jacob would go to Jerusalem and open all the Gates to the Upper Worlds and receive the power to change our world forever. The Creator and all the angels came together to observe Jacob from Above. When Jacob arrived in Jerusalem, they got very excited, but he did not stop and continued on his the way to Charan. The Creator must have been heartbroken, and all the angels disappointed. The Creator explained to the angels that if Jacob did not awaken himself to pray in Jerusalem, the Creator could not do it for him. Jacob had to awaken himself, he had to be full-hearted and committed on his own.

Once Jacob awakened himself in Charan, he realized his mistake and immediately decided to return to Jerusalem. He said, "I am going to travel all the way back to Jerusalem. I am not going to stop to rest, I am not going to stop to get a meal, I am not going to stop to relax. I have got to go and do this." At that moment, the most unbelievable miracle occurred. The Creator took Mount Moriah, the most important spiritual site in the world, and brought it all the way to Beit El. Why? What was the point?

Jacob would have traveled all the way back to Jerusalem without the miracle. The lesson for us is this: Once we make the commitment, once we make the decision, miracles will happen to us all the time. It was not necessary for the Creator to detach part of Jerusalem and bring it to Beit El. But the Creator told the angels that because Jacob was committed and had awakened himself, realized his mistake, and had the desire to correct it, the Creator needed to send him all the miracles, even the unnecessary ones, to assist him.

From this understanding, we become awakened to an alarming paradox. On the one hand, Jacob received nothing. Jacob lost everything. He walked through Jerusalem without stopping, so he did not receive all the blessings of support and the miracles that were destined to come to him. He did not receive one instant of inspiration, not one bit of assistance from the Creator. Can you imagine what would have been if Jacob had not awakened himself once he was in Charan? He would have carried on with all his spiritual work; he would have prayed all day and studied, and done everything correctly. Then he would have asked the Creator, "Why are my actions not working? Why do I not feel Your assistance?" He would never have known that it was because he did not make the commitment, that he did not awaken himself while he traveled through Jerusalem.

So, we can perform many actions but receive nothing. On the other hand, with true commitment, true awakening, we can receive all the miracles, even unnecessary ones. It is a tremendous revelation to realize how many angels, how many miracles, today, tomorrow, this week, await our awakening. The Creator is waiting. We might not be on the same spiritual level as Jacob, but there are openings, gifts, and blessings that are destined to come our way. However, these blessings and miracles cannot come to us if we do not make the commitment, if we do not create an awakening for them. We can do our spiritual work without awakening ourselves—and never understand why we do not have the assistance of the Creator.

Jacob prayed when he arrived in Charan; he performed actions and did his spiritual work, and the opening for blessings and miracles awaited him. However, there was an extra level of awakening that he needed to push himself to achieve. If we do not push to reach this extra level of awakening, nobody can do it for us, and we will receive nothing. Conversely, if we awaken ourselves—if we do not allow a day or a week to go by without realizing that there is something more we have to do—and we push ourselves in a tremendous way, everything opens up. We receive unnecessary miracles; we receive assistance from the angels, assistance from the Creator Himself because, as the Creator says, "I am going to give this person all the assistance possible because he awakened himself." The flip side of the coin is that we need to understand the danger of not pushing ourselves to achieve this awakening. Not pushing ourselves can result in complete darkness, where no Light, nothing, can become manifest.

What a beautiful lesson. When Jacob awakened himself to return to Jerusalem, when he decided he had to return and did a little work to achieve this end, the miracle occurred.

True Love

The Bible says that when Jacob arrived in Charan, he saw Rachel and he kissed her. For some of us, this story may appear to be strange. This is one of those rare times in the Torah where we find a couple who is not married and who do not even know each other, kissing. This is also the only time in the

Torah where we have a glimpse of what true love is. Jacob came to Laban and said, "I will work for you for seven years so I can marry your daughter." Laban agreed, and Jacob worked for seven years. To both Jacob and Rachel, these seven years were akin to only a few days because of their love for each other.

When we speak about love, we're talking about a much larger topic than can be covered in a lecture or chapter. However, we have to start from the understanding that what most of us view as love is not true love.

When we say, for example, that we love food, that we love fish or meat or pasta, do we really feel any love toward the meat, fish, or pasta? Of course not. We want the fish to be killed for us so that we can eat it. We want the cow slaughtered for us so that we can eat its meat. Right? But this is the way most of us view love. For most of us, our love is selfish, based on "What do I get?" This is not true love. For Jacob and Rachel, the seven years that they could not be together seemed like only a few days. What is the difference? When love is based on "what I receive," then seven years could seem like a lifetime. When it is not, seven years can feel like just a few days.

One of the gifts of the Shabbat of Vayetze is that when we ask for even a glimpse of true love, we can receive assistance to achieve true love. But we have to begin with the understanding that 99.9 percent of what we think of as true love is not love at all. It is some silly form of the *Desire to Receive for the Self Alone*. If we do not know we have a problem, we will never find the solution.

Jacob and Rachel achieved a certain level of true love, which in its ultimate form is known as the *Desire to Share*. In *Ten Luminous Emanations*, Rav Ashlag speaks about how the *Malchut*, the Vessel in the Endless World called *nekuda penimit* (internal point), is surrounded by the Light. He said, "If you viewed this internal point and all the Light that surrounds it, you would notice that this point can receive endlessly; because it does not receive the Light internally, it somehow receives the Light externally."

This is a very complicated concept. But essentially, any element of love that is attached to the *Desire to Receive for the Self Alone* is not love; it is simply selfishness. Conversely, any aspect of love that is of the *Desire to Share* is the beginning and awakening of love. Jacob and Rachel had the ability to experience true love only because of their spiritual work. Although their love was a pure love based on the Desire to Share, it had nothing to do with what either one of them could give the other. The love they shared was more of an appreciation of what each soul could do for the world. When he saw Rachel, Jacob viewed her as a channel—the chariot for Malchut. He recognized the Light that she could reveal for the world. His love for her had nothing to do with how she made him feel or what she could do for him.

Jacob's appreciation for what Rachel could and would do for the world was where his love came from. On a certain level, Jacob's love for Rachel was the same love many of us hope to achieve in our love for the Creator. The *Zohar* says that this love that is not based on what we receive for ourselves, but is called *Yirat haRomemut* (love based on appreciation). Because we have an appreciation for someone, or in this case, the Creator, this appreciation in and of itself awakens our love. Jacob and Rachel were on this level. The love they felt for one another was not love that fed any level of their *Desire to Receive for the Self Alone;* their love was based on an appreciation of who they were as channels for our world.

Therefore, for Jacob and Rachel, whether they were together right then or in seven years was not important. Jacob's love for Rachel was not based on whether she was going to make dinner for him at night or if she was going to make him happy. Rachel's love for Jacob was not based on whether he made her laugh or made her feel good. Their love for one another was based on a true appreciation for each other's soul, for who they truly were, and for what they could do for the world. On this level, it did not matter whether they were together or not because their love and appreciation for each other was beyond anything that they could receive and not dependent at all on time or space.

Most of us are far from experiencing this type of love. What we call love is really selfishness. I think that many of us make a distinction between the love that we try to awaken for the Light of the Creator and the love that we have for our friends or our spouses. But at their truest and purest, all of these forms of love are identical.

What we need to ask for on the Shabbat of Vayetze is to become awakened and to be given the ability to truly love. Our first step has to be an awareness of how far away we are from true love, along with an understanding that what we think of as love is, for the most part, simply the selfish *Desire to Receive for the Self Alone.* It is darkness. On this Shabbat, we can say to the Creator, "We know that what we think of as love is not love, but rather the *Desire to Receive for the Self Alone.* Please open up our hearts and give us the ability to awaken true love."

OUR ONLY HOPE IS TO DIMINISH OUR EGO

It is important to remember that when we speak about and study from righteous souls like Jacob or Reuben, we make a strong connection with them, just as when we study *Ten Luminous Emanations*, we connect with the souls of Rav Isaac Luria and Rav Ashlag, or when we study from the *Zohar*, we connect with Rabbi Shimon bar Yochai.

The chapter of Vayishlach opens with Jacob going to meet with his brother Esau, with whom he had not had any contact for many years. Jacob had spent many years working for Laban, his father-in-law, and was now going to meet Esau, who hated him. The Bible tells us that Jacob prayed to the Creator prior to this meeting, saying, "I feel so small from all the goodness that You, the Creator, have given me." Jacob's ego was so diminished that he felt overwhelmed by the gifts that the Creator had given him. Jacob had prepared a gift for Esau, but when he approached Esau, he bowed down seven times before him until he reached his brother.

What we learn from these two important facts in this story—that Jacob's ego was so diminished and that Jacob bowed down seven times before Esau—is that the only hope that we have to achieve what we came to this world to accomplish is to constantly diminish our ego.

The Torah says Jacob saw how strong the powers of negativity were and realized that he had to forget about prayer, forget about study, forget about spiritual work; the only hope he had of protecting himself against the negative forces was to diminish himself, diminish his ego. As he came toward Esau, he performed seven giant actions of reducing his ego. This was strenuous spiritual work, but Jacob realized at this moment that although he had prepared for a great battle with the forces of Edom, with the forces of the *Galut* (of the Exile), by coming with a gift and a prayer—only when he saw Esau, did he realize what he was truly battling against. With this awakening, this awareness, everything else went out the window. All of Jacob's spiritual work, all his prayers, all his study—none of these spiritual tools was going to help him in this battle. Jacob realized that his only hope of being victorious was to push himself down one time, push himself down a second time, a third, fourth, fifth, sixth, and finally, a seventh time.

We have to understand that diminishing our ego is not just part of our spiritual work; it is our only option for defeating negativity. Therefore, the first section of Vayishlach is

devoted to Jacob's preparations before his battle with the
negative forces.

It is written that the only way a person can rise in
righteousness, the only way a person can become a *tzadik* (a
righteous person), is if he throws himself down at least seven
times (connecting to seven different spiritual levels).

For us to truly comprehend this concept, we need to realize that
most of us are like Jacob at the beginning of this story. We have
our tools, we have our spiritual work, we have our prayers, we
have our study. We can do all the necessary preparation for our
battle against Esau, against negativity. However, all these tools
and preparation will lead to failure. Jacob made all the plans,
but if he had not truly appreciated the enormous power of the
negative forces, he would have failed and would have died.

To win the battle against negativity, we first have to truly
appreciate the magnitude of the negative force. The question
we have to ask ourselves is this: Do we realize that we have no
option for victory other than to diminish our ego?

When we realize who the Esau is in our lives, when we have a
true understanding of the forces we are fighting against, then it
becomes obvious that we need to throw all the preparation
referred to at the beginning of Vayishlach out the window and
focus only on pushing our ego down, time and time again.

Because most of us are still living our lives like the Jacob at the
beginning of this story, we need to understand that the ego is

truly terrible, that we have no other option for victory except to diminish our ego.

This is an extremely important lesson. We cannot lie to ourselves about this. The only time we can truly achieve a connection to the Light of the Creator is if we realize we do not understand what we are fighting against, nor have we any appreciation of the extent of our battle with the negative forces. Everything we thought would save us from Esau, everything we thought would save us from the forces of darkness—none of this will assist us to achieve victory.

This is the key. What we truly need to internalize from this story is that diminishing our ego is our only option.

BECOMING LIKE GOD

There are three other elements that I would like to discuss regarding the diminishment of our ego. The famous battle between Jacob and the angel took place the night before Jacob met with Esau. When describing Jacob's spiritual level prior to meeting the angel, the Torah uses the word *levado,* which means "alone." The *Midrash* explains that this term is used in reference to Jacob to indicate that he was by himself. Being alone is not a simple level to achieve.

There is no one like the Creator. No one can be like God, with the exception of certain people who through their spiritual work can attain the same level as God. Every power that the Creator possesses, a *tzadik* (righteous person) can possess, and each one of us needs to aspire to attain this level of power as well. Just as the Creator can resurrect the dead, so too, can Elijah the Prophet resurrect the dead. The Creator can make something small become a great blessing, and so can Elijah the Prophet. The Creator can give a blessing to a barren woman to have children, and Elisha the Prophet also had that power. The Creator has the power to sweeten what is bitter, and so too, could Elisha the Prophet sweeten what was bitter.

"There is no one like God" is a statement that encompasses most people, but there are a few exceptions—people who can merit attaining the level of God. Jacob was one such person. When the Bible says that Jacob was left alone, it is to indicate that he achieved the level of the Creator. Jacob achieved the level of *levado*, of possessing all the power of the Creator.

In Avodat Israel, Rabbi Israel of Koshnitz explains how we can we achieve the level of God, how we can have the ability to create miracles. He says the only way we can attain a complete connection to the Creator and reach the level of God is by achieving the spiritual level of *Ayin* (nothingness), a complete diminishment of ego. The level of *Ayin* is where we realize we are nothing in our own eyes: We become humble and neither care for nor worry about ourselves. Through a true diminishment of our ego and a complete annihilation of our own selfish desires, we connect completely to the Essence of the Light of the Creator. When a person attains this level of connection to the Creator, he or she achieves the ability to decree miracles, blessings, and even redemption, as desired.

If there is judgment, God forbid, that is decreed, someone on this level of *Ayin* (nothingness) has the ability to transform this judgment. When we are on the level of nothingness, we can take any judgment, make it null and void, and change it into a blessing.

We spoke previously about the primary lesson from Jacob, which is that the only way we can ever hope to achieve what we came to this world to achieve is to constantly repress, constantly throw down our ego.

The Avodat Israel reveals the second important aspect of diminishing our ego: that we cannot awaken real blessings, we cannot awaken real transformation, we cannot transform judgment into mercy unless we achieve this level of *Ayin*, this level of nothingness. However, if we do make attaining this level of *Ayin* the focus of our spiritual work, then we can realize all these blessings.

Much of our work at The Kabbalah Centre is devoted to reaching many people and sharing the wisdom of Kabbalah with them, which, of course, is important. But for those of us who truly understand this concept, our focus needs to be on striving to truly achieve this level of *Ayin*. The *Zohar*, in *Noach*, says if there are ten people in complete unity, *Mashiach* will come. What does this mean? Complete unity can only be attained when ten people have achieved the level of *Ayin*, complete nothingness, complete annihilation of the ego.

We can either strive to reach a critical mass of people in the world, whatever that number is, or we can focus on only ten people and get these ten people to completely annihilate their egos.

Maybe this is what we should be focusing on—I do not know—but regardless of what we do with this knowledge, clearly we have to make sure that we do not get lost in "teaching" our students and thus lose this important idea. Achieving the level of *Ayin* is not an addendum to or in addition to our spiritual work. If I want to have the ability to awaken blessings, if I want to have the ability to transform judgment into mercy, I have to be singularly focused on achieving this level of *Ayin*.

If we can, on a scale of one to ten—ten being *Ayin* and one being completely ego-driven—move one degree closer towards *Ayin*, then the Light that goes forth from us is much more powerful than reaching another hundred or even another five hundred people. This does not mean that we should strive to do one thing and not the other, but it certainly means that we should try not to lose sight of our focus on the attainment of nothingness while we are reaching more people. As the *Zohar* says, if ten people achieve true *Ayin*, true nothingness, *Mashiach* will come. So if we help two hundred people achieve fifty percent of *Ayin*, it may not bring *Mashiach*, but at least it brings the world much, that much closer. All too often, we lose awareness that whatever we are doing cannot compare to this achievement of *Ayin*, to our achievement of nothingness.

IF WE DIMINISH OURSELVES, JUDGMENT CANNOT COME

A third understanding of the level of *Ayin* is presented in Rabban Gamliel's tale in the *Talmud: Yevamot:* "Once I was on a boat and passed by another boat that had been destroyed. I was worried because I knew the passengers on that boat. I knew Rabbi Akiva was on the boat. I thought that maybe, God forbid, Rabbi Akiva had died in that boat wreck. When I got off my boat and I saw Rabbi Akiva was teaching, I went over to him and asked, 'How did you survive the boat wreck?' Rabbi Akiva answered me, 'You want to know how I survived the destruction of the boat? I grabbed onto one of the planks of wood from the boat that was destroyed and floated on the ocean. As the great waves came to take me under, I bent my head down. Every time a huge wave came to take me under, I bent my head down.'"

It is from this story that the sages understood that if, God forbid, a negative person or any type of judgment is approaching, then, like Jacob, they should bend their head down.

WHAT GOD MEANT
～ Vayishlach ～

The Maharal (Rabbi Loew ben Bezalel, 1502–1609) explains
that what we learn from this is if a person diminishes himself,
judgment cannot come to him. It is simple spiritual logic. If
you are nobody, then judgment cannot come to you because
you are not there. If you are somebody, God forbid, judgment
can come. Rabbi Akiva understood this truth, so whenever the
waves came toward him to drown him, he ducked his head, or
annihilated his ego. Thanks to this annihilation of his ego, he
survived the waves. This is the same lesson we learned from
Jacob's example: Every time Jacob saw the negative power of
Esau coming toward him, he bowed down. As the Maharal
points out, when a person is "not there," the forces of
negativity cannot attach to him.

IF WE DO NOT BELIEVE WE DESERVE, WE DO NOT LOSE ANY LIGHT

There is one more lesson concerning Jacob and the diminishing
of ego that I would like share with you. As mentioned
previously, Jacob said to the Creator, "I am diminished because
of all Your kindness." The *Midrash* explains that Jacob was
afraid that if the Creator saved him from Esau, his merits (or
whatever Light Jacob had created for himself) would be taken
away as a payment for the Creator having saved him. The
Midrash goes on to say that the reason none of Jacob's Light was
taken away from him was because Jacob believed he did not
deserve to be saved. This is important spiritual logic.

If, when we wake up in the morning, we think we deserve to wake up, the Creator will say, "You have a hundred levels of Light, so when you wake up in the morning, which you know you deserve, I will take away one level." As the day progresses, we have an opportunity to receive enjoyment from something and we consciously or unconsciously say, "I deserve this." To this, the Creator will say, "You are correct, now you have ninety-nine levels of Light, and I have to take one level away as a payment because you feel you deserve this enjoyment." And so on and so forth. To the degree we think we deserve whatever we receive, the Creator says, "You are correct, but because you think you deserve, I will have to take away a level of your Light."

Conversely, imagine a person who wakes up in the morning and says, "I really do not deserve to wake up in the morning; I really do not deserve to have this blessing from the Creator. In fact, I really do not deserve to have what I have." This cannot be a game, however! When you truly believe and say this, the Creator answers, "You know what? You are right, but I will give Light to you as *Chesed*, as a kindness for no reason. No Light will be taken away from you for whatever you truly believe you do not deserve." This is a very important spiritual logic to understand.

Jacob said, "I do not deserve to be saved from Esau." If Jacob thought that he had banked enough Light, enough merit, to save himself, then Light would be taken out of his "account." How was Jacob saved from Esau without having to give payment for it, without a diminishment of his Light? Jacob was saved from Esau because he truly believed that he did not deserve to be saved.

If we believe we do not deserve to receive and say to the Creator, "I do not deserve this. You are giving this to me even though I do not deserve it," who pays for what is received? The Creator pays for it, not us. But if the Creator gives us something and we believe we deserve it, we have to pay for it. We have to pay for it with our Light. This is a tremendous lesson for us.

CORRECT ACTION, WRONG CONSCIOUSNESS

When Jacob met with Esau, Jacob introduced his entire family to his brother. The Bible says that when Jacob brought his family to Esau, he placed the handmaids, Bilhah and Zilpah in the front with their children, and behind them, he placed Leah and her children, and at the rear, he put Rachel and Joseph.

The *Midrash* asks where Dina, Jacob's only daughter, was. It goes on to explain that Jacob was afraid that if Esau saw Dina, he would want to marry her, so not wanting Dina to marry Esau, Jacob hid her in a chest.

The *Midrash* writes that Jacob brought judgment on himself through this incident. The *Midrash* explains that judgment was awakened because Jacob locked Dina in the chest and did not allow Esau to see her. If Esau would have seen Dina, there is a good possibility he would have married her, and if he would have married her, maybe he would have changed his ways. But because Jacob did not give Esau this opportunity to transform, terrible events transpired.

How do we make sense of this statement of the *Midrash*?

Those of us who have children can identify with Jacob's decision; Esau was a terribly negative person, and therefore, Jacob did the right thing. Clearly, he did not want his daughter to marry Esau, so he hid her away. Why did such judgment come to Jacob from this action?

There are two thoughts I would like to share concerning this incident. One famous explanation says that Jacob was correct in hiding Dina in the chest, but he made a mistake as he did so. The words used to describe this mistake are: "He closed the lock too strong." What does this mean? Sometimes when we have to do something and we know it is the proper thing to do, we do it. The question, however, is this: "What are we feeling when we perform this action? What is our true emotion behind this action?"

Every so often, opportunities arise for us to help someone realize their mistakes. The question we need to ask ourselves is whether we enjoy telling this person what his or her faults are or whether we feel pain. "Does it hurt me as much as it hurts the person whom I have upset, even though I know it is the right thing to do?"

Our action will be the same in both cases: We will tell them exactly the same thing in exactly the same way, but what are we feeling inside? Are we in terrible pain because we have to do this, or do we enjoy it?

Here is an example to better illustrate this point. A man has mice in his house. He decides to get rid of the mice, so he purchases a cat to eat the mice. The action of getting rid of the mice is the same for the man and the cat. The only difference between them is that the owner of the house only wants to get rid of the mice; the cat, however, enjoys killing the mice. The man and the cat have a completely different consciousness behind their action.

Jacob was correct in hiding Dina. However, when we go into the details of the story, we realize that there was a chance that if Esau had married Dina, he might have become a *tzadik*, a righteous person. But let us assume that Jacob did the correct thing: that he closed Dina in the chest because he wanted to save her from Esau, and it was the right thing to do.

Then the question to ask is: What was Jacob thinking when he put Dina inside the chest? Did he think, "I feel so bad; I wish that Dina could marry my brother and could make him righteous and turn him around," or did he even think of Esau at all? Did Jacob think only, "I'm going to protect my daughter?" Because Jacob's focus was on "I'm going to protect my daughter," and not about feeling the pain of his brother judgment came to Jacob. This is a difference in thought, not in action.

Story: Feeling the Pain of the Animal

In the *Talmud* there is a story about Rabbi Yehuda HaNassi and a little animal that was to be slaughtered for food.

The animal came crying and hid near Rabbi Yehuda. The animal was making sad noises because it knew that it was about to be slaughtered and it did not want to be killed.

Rabbi Yehuda told the animal, "Go to be slaughtered; this is what you are created for." The *Talmud* then says something frightening: "Because Rabbi Yehuda did not have mercy on this animal, the Heavens decreed that judgment and pain would come to him, and for thirteen years, Rabbi Rav Yehuda suffered great pain." We have to understand we are talking about the Rabbi Yehuda of the *Talmud*, a very elevated soul.

Once again, Rabbi Yehuda was correct in what he said: Animals are in this world for us to eat them so that the sparks of Light within them can be elevated. The point is not whether he said the right words or the wrong words; the point was whether he felt badly for the animal when he spoke to it. This is vital. It is more dangerous to do what is correct than to do what is wrong because we may never wake from it.

What we should learn from Jacob is that we can do all the right things, but if our feelings, our consciousness behind our action are not one of caring, then, God forbid, this action could lead to tremendous judgment. This is an extremely important lesson.

Story: Saving Souls

One night, I was reading with my son, David, about Rabbi
Naftali of Rufshitz who was at one time a student of Rabbi
Mordechai Neshchiz. Rabbi Naftali was very close to his
teacher and spent all the holidays with him. One year during
Purim, Rabbi Mordechai informed his student that he did not
want to spend the coming Passover with him. Rabbi Naftali
was hurt and upset and asked his teacher what he could do to
change his teacher's mind.

His teacher did not answer him.

Rabbi Naftali truly wanted to spend Passover with his teacher,
so he conjured up a plan. He decided, a few weeks before the
holiday, to make himself indispensable to the wife of Rabbi
Mordechai. Rabbi Naftali helped her in the kitchen preparing
the food for *Passover*. By being indispensable, he believed that
this would ensure that she would invite him to stay for the
Passover Seder.

Rabbi Mordechai's wife was so grateful for Rabbi Naftali's
assistance with the preparation of the food for the Passover
Seder that she said, "I truly could not have done all this
cooking without your help, thank you so much."

The day before Passover, Rabbi Naftali informed her that he
needed to leave and make his way to his home as he would not
be spending Passover with her and Rabbi Mordechai. He
thanked her for the opportunity of helping her and told her it

was a true pleasure to assist her with all the preparations. Rabbi Mordechai's wife turned to him and said, "How can you leave me now? I still need your help." Rabbi Naftali replied, "Of course, I would love to stay and continue helping you, but your husband, my teacher, said that it would not be possible for me to spend Passover with him and his family this year."

So she went to her husband and said, "I know you told Rabbi Naftali that he cannot stay with us for Passover, but I truly cannot do it without his help. I'm begging you, please, let him stay." Her husband conceded, "If it is that important to you, I will let him stay, but I believe that he is going to make tremendous trouble for me."

The morning before the Passover *Seder*, they burned the *chametz* (leavened bread), and Rabbi Naftali began to feel the Light of Passover approaching. He went to the *mikveh* (ritual bathhouse) and immersed himself in the waters, then went to the hall of study, to study and prepare to elevate himself higher before the Passover *Seder*. While Rabbi Naftali sat and studied, a man walked in and approached him, as he was the only person there at the time. The man asked him, "Can you show me where Rabbi Mordechai Neshchiz lives? I would like to speak to him before Passover." Spiritually elevated people have a heightened sense of smell, so when this man walked into the hall of study, Rabbi Naftali smelled him and not only did he stink physically, but he also stank spiritually—his soul was filthy.

In reply to this request, Rabbi Naftali said, "How dare you think to go and talk to my teacher before Passover? Do you know how elevated he is on this day? Now leave." Rabbi Naftali practically threw the man out of the hall. Five minutes had gone by when Rabbi Mordechai entered, walked straight up to Rabbi Naftali, and asked, "Did anybody come to study besides you? Has anyone else been here?" To which Rabbi Naftali replied, "No, nobody significant has been here for a long time. I have been sitting alone."

Rabbi Mordechai asked him again, "Has anybody been here in the past fifteen minutes?" Sensing his teacher's concern, Rabbi Naftali replied, "Well, you know, there was a man, a terribly negative person, filthy both physically and spiritually, who asked to see you, but I told him that he should not waste your time."

His teacher looked at him and said, "If you do not bring that person to me right now, you are never going to see me again."

Distressed by the outrage of his teacher, Rabbi Naftali rushed out of the hall of study and wandered all through town, searching for the man. He could not find him. Ultimately, as a last resort, he decided to go to the tavern to see if the man was there. Sure enough, he saw the man, filthy drunk, sitting at the bar. Rabbi Naftali went up to him and said, "I'm so sorry, my teacher wants to see you. Please, will you let me show you where he lives? He really wants to see you."

The drunken man relied, "Do you know how much you embarrassed me? There is no way I will come with you." Rabbi Naftali begged him, "If you do not come with me now to my teacher, I'm finished. My teacher swore that I am never going to see his face again if I do not bring you to him now." And with that, Rabbi Naftali picked the drunken man up, put him over his shoulder, and carried him to his teacher.

The holiday of Passover began and Rabbi Naftali was seated somewhere in the back of the hall of study, while this filthy man—who, although he had bathed, was still a spiritually low soul—stood right next to Rabbi Mordechai throughout the prayers. At the Passover *Seder*, again Rabbi Mordechai sat right next to this man, and again Rabbi Naftali was seated all the way at the other end of the table. His teacher did not even say hello to him, nothing; he ignored Rabbi Naftali not only for the *Seder* but also for the entire holiday.

As a result, Rabbi Naftali had a very difficult Passover. At the end of the holiday, he approached his teacher to beg for forgiveness, and his teacher said, "I want to tell you who this man is. Long ago, I had a very close student, who was with me for many years. However, at one point he fell and continued falling until he was very low spiritually. It has been maybe fifteen years since he originally fell, and he has only gotten worse. Before this holiday of Passover, I saw in a vision that there was some awakening of repentance, some awakening of purification within him. My student thought, 'I will go to my teacher one last time. And if he takes me in, then I will know that there is still hope for my soul. But if this opening is closed, if I do not get to see my teacher, I will know my life is over.'

"Knowing how spiritual and pure you are, I knew that if you were here with me during this Passover, you would mess up this opportunity of correction for this incredible soul. This is why I asked you not to be here. You, however, found a way to be with me and the rest you know. This was his last chance to redeem himself. You saw that he was a filthy nobody who did not even deserve to come to me before Passover, and you were correct. But had he not been given this opportunity, you would have killed his soul forever."

What we learn from this story is that we often see the truth concerning someone. But we can never forget that we are dealing with souls, and so we need to truly appreciate how careful we have to be.

Judgment came down to Jacob, even though Jacob was correct—Esau was filthy. But before Jacob gave up on his brother's soul, he should have left a little opening for the possibility of transformation. This is an extremely important lesson for us, especially for those of us who are teaching and helping people. We never truly know the effect of our actions on another's soul or how the words we utter sound to the soul we are speaking to. When we take it upon ourselves to be responsible for someone else's soul in one capacity or another, we must truly appreciate the magnitude of that responsibility.

On some level, Jacob fell short with Esau and thereby brought down tremendous judgment upon himself. In the story of Rabbi Naftali of Rufshitz, he almost killed the former student of his rabbi forever. If this opening for the man to correct had not been left open, the man would have died for a long time. Hopefully, we will all become awakened by the examples of

Jacob and Rabbi Naftali of Rufshitz to appreciate the type fear we should have and care we must take when dealing with people's souls.

Vayeshev

WHAT WE THINK OF OURSELVES IS THE LIGHT THAT WE DRAW

The Bible says after the brothers had sold Joseph, Yehuda, who was truly the leader at that point, stepped down because he realized that he had made a mistake. He stepped down, married, and had children. Yehuda's first two children were evil, but then he had one more son. The sages explain that within this simple story lies the birth of the seed of *Mashiach*, the birth of the seed of the removal of chaos, pain, suffering and death from our world.

The *Mei HaShiloach* (*Living Waters* by Rav Mordechai Yosef Leiner of Izbica, 1801–1854) poses the question: "If Yehuda realized he had done something wrong, would he not want to work on himself spiritually?" So why did he get married immediately after he realized his mistake in leading the brothers to sell Joseph? The answer is that Yehuda saw the pain that his father, Jacob, was experiencing. It was Yehuda who brought Joseph's blood-stained clothing to his father. Jacob asked, "Is this Joseph's coat?" to which Yehuda replied, "Yes." Because this caused such trauma to his father, Yehuda's consciousness fell. Yehuda now believed that all hope was gone for him in his life.

Yehuda got married because he truly believed that his spiritual life was over and there was nothing that he could, or would, accomplish in this lifetime. However, if he had children, they could do something good, perhaps even awaken a correction in this world. Therefore, Yehuda's consciousness when he decided to get married was based on his giving up hope on himself, and believing that his children would do something to awaken the Light of correction.

Yehuda named his first son Er (meaning, "to awaken") in the hope that Er would awaken the Light of the Creator. Er, however, was not a good person. Can you imagine? Yehuda, believing that there was no hope for himself, decides to have children, only to discover that they are not good people?

The Creator made Yehuda understand in no uncertain terms: "If you think that you have no hope, that you have no spiritual life in your soul; if you really believe that you have no hope, that you have no connection to the Light of the Creator, you could have a hundred children and it is not going to make any difference because you cannot give them more than you are. They will not be able to do anything positive in this world."

In the *Ten Luminous Emanations*, Rav Isaac Luria (the Ari) explains that whatever Light comes down from the Creator to our world has to come through a channel, or conduit. If the conduit does not believe that he or she has the ability to fulfill this role, then the children he or she will have will also lack that ability.

What we learn from this insightful teaching is the reason that Yehuda's children, Er and Onan, were so negative, was because Yehuda's consciousness of "I am worthless" was passed on to his children. Whatever we think of ourselves is the Light that we will manifest.

The Mei HaShiloach continues: "Only after Yehuda understood this concept and truly internalized it, thereby re-awakening the consciousness within him of 'I must believe that I can accomplish; I must believe that I have the ability,' he had another son, whom he named Shelah. The name 'Shelah' comes from the concept of making a mistake. What Yehuda implied by this name was that he understood he had made a mistake with his first two children and he wanted to correct that mistake with this child. Therefore, Yehuda's first two children did not remain alive, while Shelah did."

This is a very important lesson for us in all that we do, not just with our children but with our friends and with anything we want to manifest. We cannot manifest anything that we do not believe we are capable of manifesting. To better understand this concept, imagine that we have a meter that registers hopelessness/hopefulness. On one end, there is complete hope, complete certainty that the Redemption (the end of pain and suffering) will come, and on the other end (where Yehuda was) lies complete hopelessness. Most of us fall somewhere on this continuum.

If, God forbid, a person wakes up in the morning and his consciousness is at the level of Yehuda's consciousness—complete hopelessness—this is the energy he will inject into his children and friends. Someone like this can drag all the people he loves and cares about all the way down.

Indeed, if we wake up one morning and have a little certainty mixed in with even a little hopelessness, all the Light we wish to transfer will not be able to be transferred.

It is important to understand that every day of our lives that we are giving over wisdom or devoting to creativity or hoping to manifest, the level of trust and belief that we have in our ability to be a conduit for the Light of the Creator determines how much we can transfer to our child, student, or idea we wish to manifest. We can make the exact same connection on two different days, but if on one day we have less certainty about our ability to transfer Light, and on the second day we have more certainty, we will give more Light on the second day.

The Mei HaShiloach says that we as channels either diminish or increase the Light of the Creator, depending on how much certainty we have in ourselves. Because Yehuda truly believed that he had nothing, he dropped all the way down to the point where he thought he could not be a channel at all for the Light of the Creator. That is why he put his hope in what his children would create, in what this next generation would create. But these children did not create anything. We cannot create, nor can we transfer to a friend or a child, something that we do not have complete certainty in our ability to create or transfer. What we have to awaken from this lesson is the importance and necessity of strengthening our certainty in our ability to be conduits for the Light of the Creator. The degree to which we have certainty in our ability to be a channel for the Light of the Creator determines how much Light we can transfer to others or manifest in our lives.

What makes a difference is not what we say, what we teach, what we transfer, but rather where our certainty is regarding our ability to be a channel. To the degree that we have more certainty in our ability to be a conduit for the Light of the Creator, is how much Light we transfer. This is a very important principle to understand.

The other side of this coin is that there is always a danger that in approaching certainty, we may fall prey to overconfidence and ego, thinking, "I am so smart, so spiritual," rather than being a true and simple conduit for the Light of the Creator. Yes, we're striving for complete certainty, but when we think that "I" can give over or "I" can channel, we fall into the realm of ego-driven, or negative, consciousness. One aspect of negative thinking is that we cannot be a conduit for the Light of the Creator, and the other side of the same coin (where many teachers tend to go) is thinking and believing that our wisdom, our understanding, our ability to share spiritual Light is the key. This, too, leads to darkness.

GREATER THINGS ARE HAPPENING

In one of my favorite sections in *Midrash Rabba*, *Vayeshev*, Rabbi Shmuel, the son of Nachman, quoting a verse from Jeremiah says, "The Creator says, 'I know people's thoughts.' The tribes, the brothers, were busy with the sale of Joseph, and Joseph was busy with his depression and sadness. Reuben was busy with his sadness. Jacob was busy with his sadness. Yehuda was busy getting married and dealing with his sadness. All these amazing spiritual channels were busy with their own issues, and what was the Creator doing at that moment? The Creator was creating the seed for *Mashiach* (Messiah), the seed of the *Gemar HaTikkun* (Final Redemption)."

What we understand from this *Midrash* is that so many times when we are busy with our own feelings, being upset or sad about something or someone—when we are lost in all this stupidity and silliness—we lose sight of the miraculous process that is occurring in the bigger picture. When we are busy with this silliness, we detach ourselves from the ability to be connected to the miraculous processes in our lives. Here we have two realities occurring at the same time: We have the reality where Joseph, Reuben, Yehuda, and Jacob are all worried, depressed, and sad, and a second reality in which the Creator is manifesting the seed for King David, the seed for the *Gemar HaTikkun*.

When we embed ourselves in our own silly stuff, we detach ourselves from the true process that is occurring at the same time—the creation of the seed of the *Gemar HaTikkun.* This detachment from the miraculous process of the Final Redemption, caused by allowing ourselves to fall into our silliness, is our first important insight from this Midrash.

"I Lift Up My Soul to You"

The Mei HaShiloach explains that King David taught another important lesson. Just as a new-born baby knows that she is going to be fed by her mother (that is, knowing where and how her needs will be fulfilled), so too, when that person grows up, it is still necessary that she maintain the simple certainty that assistance comes from the Creator.

King David was of the consciousness—he believed and had complete knowledge—that he had no ability to fulfill his needs on his own. The only way to bring the Redemption, the *Gemar HaTikkun,* closer to us is to realize and understand that there is nothing that we can do on our own about it: "There is nothing that I can do; therefore, I put my complete certainty and trust in the Creator." When we come to the point where we acknowledge with a pure heart and consciousness that we know that there is nothing that we can accomplish on our own, and we have complete certainty that the Creator can bring the Redemption, then the Redemption can come quickly.

Joseph, Reuben, even Jacob were absorbed in their own work because they believed they could awaken the Redemption through their own work. But Yehuda realized there was nothing he could do on his own to correct himself, to bring about the *Gemar HaTikkun*, and he cried to the Creator time and again, "I lift up my soul to You, the Creator, because I know that only You can correct it. I cannot correct it. I know that the only hope I have is to have children because I myself cannot correct my soul."

The Mei HaShiloach explains that it was not only Yehuda's thought processes but also his spiritual work that brought him to this understanding: "I lift up my soul to You, the Creator, because I know that I cannot correct my soul on my own." The Creator said, "You are the one—not Jacob who is busy with his own correction, not Joseph who is busy with his own correction, not Reuben who is busy with his own correction— only you, Yehuda, who cries day and night saying, 'I cannot do this by myself. I lift up my soul to You, the Creator, and I beg, please fix it for me because I cannot fix it myself.' You are the one who will bring *Mashiach*. You are the one who will plant the seed for *Mashiach*."

It is a paradox. Yehuda's understanding of "I cannot do anything; I am hopeless, but I know that You, the Creator, can do the correction" was the very quality that brought him close to the Creator. Not only close, but his seemingly negative mindset allowed Yehuda to be the one who could and would bring the seed of Redemption.

There are two lessons we learn from Yehuda. First, when Yehuda believed there was nothing he could do and he gave up hope completely, his two sons died. His lack of certainty put an end to his ability to draw down the Light. Second, when he came to realize that although it was true that he was hopeless on his own and there was nothing that he could do to correct his soul, he realized he could lift up his soul to the Creator and say, "Please, because You can fix it, will You fix it?"

What we learn from this is that the only way to bring the Redemption, for ourselves personally and for the world, is first to know that we cannot do it on our own, and second to beg and yell and cry to the Creator, "You fix it! You fix my soul; You bring the Redemption." We cannot have one without the other, though. For most of us, our ego convinces us that we can take action to make the Redemption happen. Jacob, Reuben, and Joseph were all busy taking action, busy correcting; it was only Yehuda who came to the realization there was nothing that he could do on his own, so he cried again and again to the Creator, "You have to fix my soul."

The Creator only Gives Necessities

Rav Ashlag says the Creator does not give us additional gifts; the Creator gives us only what we need. Can you imagine a homeless person approaching you and saying, "I would like to buy a cashmere overcoat; can you give me some money?" Your first reaction would most probably be to laugh and walk away. However, if the same homeless person approached you and said, "I need some bread, I'm hungry," you are more likely to give him money and not send him away empty-handed.

The Creator is the same way. If we come to the Creator and say, "I am doing a lot of work and I really think I am accomplishing a lot, but it would be really nice if You could give me a little help," the Creator does not help. But when we come to the Creator, time and time again, knowing truly in our heart and soul that there is nothing we can do, and say, "Please, I beg of You, correct my soul, bring the Redemption," this awakens the assistance of the Creator, both for our own personal redemption and for global Redemption.

There is an enormous danger of becoming comfortable in our exile, of becoming comfortable in our work, where we feel satisfaction in our efforts to correct, to grow, and to accomplish. Jacob, Reuben, and Joseph did accomplish many things—way beyond anything we could ever hope to accomplish—but none of their work would plant the seed that would lead to the Redemption. Only the work of Yehuda accomplished this because he really understood that there was nothing that he could do on his own, and he cried and begged, "I ask You, I beg You, please correct my soul; please bring the seed of Redemption."

It is easy for us to fall into the trap of being satisfied with our spiritual growth, with the work we are doing, with what we are accomplishing. Although it is important that we continue this work for many reasons, not the least of which is for the process of our soul's correction, we should never lose sight of the fact that this is not the answer. It is important on the Shabbat of Vayeshev to ask for the assistance of Yehuda to reach the level of consciousness whereby "I give over my soul to the Creator. I know that there is nothing I can accomplish, but I beg You, the Creator. I know that You can do it."

Only when we are awakened to the awareness that there is nothing that we can do and we truly beg the Creator for what we need (because we know there is no other way for us to receive it), can the Creator give us our own personal correction and give us the seed, if not the ultimate Final Redemption, the complete *Geulah*.

ACHIEVING LONG LIFE BY SEEING ONLY GOOD

There is one more idea I would like to address. Joseph and his brothers did not get along. One of the reasons they did not get along was because Joseph would tell Jacob all the things he saw his brothers do wrong. In the beginning of this story, the Bible says that Jacob told Joseph, "Go to where they [Joseph's brothers] are and then come back and tell me about them." The Tiferet Shlomo (Rabbi Shlomo Hakohen of Radomsk, 1803 – 1866) says something beautiful: "We learn from this verse how dangerous it is to see bad in another person, to speak badly of another person. We see the flip side of this from *Psalms 34:12:* "Who is the man who desires life, who loves day, to see good..." where the literal translation says: "He will live a long life to see goodness." What is the secret to having a long life? Seeing only the good in other people. Who is the person who desires life? It is the person who sees only the good in others. If we want to have length of days in this world, we must make sure that we look for only the good in others. Why? There is a spiritual science (a Universal Law) to this. When a person speaks badly about another or about the bad in another person, he falls prey to the forces of negativity.

Both the *Zohar* and the *Midrash* explain that when the Creator wanted to create our world, He asked the angels, "What do you think? Should we create man or should we not create man?" There was a group of angels that said, "Do not create man; he is going to sin. You should not create humanity." Although those angels were on a very elevated level and correct in their criticism of humanity, nevertheless they fell. These Supernal Angels fell because, although they were correct, they saw something wrong in humankind. They were correct in what they said to the Creator, but poison enters us when we see the bad in another person. My father, the Rav, says that according to medical science, genetic triggers for cancer lie dormant within most people, if not all of us. What science does not understand is why this disease becomes awakened in some people and not in others. The Tiferet Shlomo explains that we unlock the dormant poison of death within us when we see the bad in others. Whether this is a conscious or unconscious thought or action does not make a difference. There is no way around it: Once we see the bad in someone, the poison is unlocked. Think about it: It was the job of the angels to come to the Creator and offer their opinions on whether or not to create humanity. To say "Do not create humanity" was not a sin (angels have no free will and thus cannot sin), and it was not a punishment that these angels fell. They fell because of the workings of a Universal Spiritual Law. Their falling was an effect of their seeing the bad in humanity. They awakened the dormant poisonous power of death in them and they fell—there was no way around it.

In another example, from the Bible, Yerovam told King Solomon all the things that he noticed the king did incorrectly, and for this criticism, Yerovam fell spiritually. Once again, this was not about punishment; it concerned the Universal Law of Cause and Effect. If we look into darkness, we awaken darkness within ourself. The Supernal Angels performed an action that had an automatic spiritual reaction. Look into darkness, God forbid, and awaken the darkness within.

The Tiferet Shlomo explains that all of us have, God willing, both a physical and a spiritual protection that the Creator has embedded within us. However, if we think badly or speak badly about another person, the Creator removes His protection from us. To take this a little deeper, once we take our protection for granted and act in ways that harm others, the Creator says, "Okay, I will remove your protection."

It is vital that we realize that the only reason we may be different from any person we are judging, is because the Creator happens to be helping us, not because we are in any way better than that other person. If we look at another person and judge him, seeing his darkness without this consciousness, we are in fact saying that we are better than he is because of ourselves, not because the Creator is protecting us. When that happens, the Creator says, "Oh, so you think you do not have any extra special protection preventing you from falling to where that person fell? You think that your own well-being is thanks to your own innate power? I'll take away the protection that I've been giving you thus far, and let's see just how far you fall without that protection!" God forbid.

A person does two things when he sees darkness in another person: He, God forbid, awakens the dormant darkness within himself, and he also removes the spiritual and physical protection from the Creator that keeps him from falling.

Only when we do not look at the darkness within another person will we be able to see the good. Jacob saw the prophecy: He knew that Joseph was in great danger of being sold into Egypt as a slave and having to experience years of pain and suffering for himself and his entire family. For that reason, Jacob said, "Please, Joseph, you are right and you are righteous. Everything you see that is negative about your brothers is a hundred percent correct, but please go and see their perfection. Please, please," he begged his son, "there is a spiritual consequence to being right and seeing what is wrong in other people. I see what is going to happen. You are going to cause pain and suffering for me, for yourself, and for all of your brothers. There is only one hope. Please go and see the perfection of your brothers. Do not see anything wrong with them. This is our only hope, Joseph."

But unfortunately, Joseph did not do obey his father, as we know. Joseph found his brothers in the field but was not yet capable of seeing the perfection in them. And thus, many years of pain and suffering followed. What a remarkably practical lesson!

If we desire life, both physical and spiritual life, we have to force ourselves to see only the good in others. This is how we protect ourselves, this is how we keep those dormant forces of physical and spiritual darkness from ever being awakened, and this is how we keep the protection of the Light of the Creator within us.

Miketz

REDEMPTION IN AN INSTANT

The story of Vayeshev, the Bible story that precedes the story of Miketz, ends with a tremendous amount of sadness. Jacob had lost his beloved son, Joseph, and was in mourning. Joseph's brothers had tried to do everything that they could to lighten the burden of their father's sadness, but they were unsuccessful. Joseph, who had been sold into slavery in Egypt and then thrown into jail where he remained for ten years, was also in a sad situation.

At the start of the Miketz, after Joseph had served an additional two years in prison, Pharaoh had two dreams. These dreams were truly the beginning of Joseph's elevation. Pharaoh's head wine steward, who had met Joseph when both men were in prison, remembered that Joseph knew how to interpret dreams, so the wine steward had Joseph pulled out of prison and brought before Pharaoh. At Pharaoh's request, Joseph successfully revealed the underlying meaning of the dreams, and Pharaoh showed his appreciation by appointing Joseph his second-in-command, helping to rule over all of Egypt.

The kabbalists draw our attention to the terrible sadness that exists at the end of Vayeshev and the tremendous joy and elevation that occurs at the beginning of Miketz. In doing so, they underscore the speed with which the joy and elevation came to pass.

Genesis 41:14 is the verse in Miketz that describes how quickly Joseph was released from the jail. After hearing that Joseph was a very good interpreter of dreams, Pharaoh sent his soldiers in attendance to "quickly run Joseph form the jail" so that he could come and prepare himself to see Pharaoh. This idea of "being run quickly" is an important teaching for us today: When assistance comes from Above, it comes quickly. There's a verse that says: "assistance from the Creator comes in a blink of an eye." This is a concept that we have to internalize and truly make a part of our consciousness.

Often when we are in a difficult situation and need assistance, we use our spiritual tools and we open ourselves up and ask for assistance from the Light of the Creator. But what we do not awaken often enough is the understanding that the assistance can—and most likely will—come in a second. Too often, we allow ourselves to accept the idea that the process is going to take time, that although the change that we are looking for will come, there is yet a process that we need to go through.

Miketz awakens within us the understanding that no, the assistance can come, and will come, in the blink of an eye.

In speaking about "they ran him quickly form the jail," the kabbalists quote a very powerful verse from *Isaiah 60:1:* "Rise, shine, for your Light has come, and the Light of the Creator shines upon you." The sages recommend we use this verse whenever we feel down, whenever we feel that we need assistance. We have to remember Joseph was at his lowest ebb, but in one second, "they ran him quickly from the jail" to the highest elevation: second-in-command of all Egypt.

We need to know that at any given moment, Light is here for us, and the Light is ready to shine upon us. Redemption, assistance from the Light of the Creator, comes in the blink of an eye: "Rise, shine, for your Light has come, and the Light of the Creator shines upon you" can occur in an instant if our consciousness is prepared for it. The first awakening, the first Light, the first lesson we want to draw from Miketz is clarity about the speed of redemption, that from the tremendous low that existed at the end of Vayeshev—where Jacob was in mourning, his children were in pain, and Joseph was sentenced to jail for ten years—in one instant, "they ran him quickly from the jail."

It is imperative that we understand that when we find ourselves imprisoned in a low level, we not think, "Even if I succeed in drawing the assistance of the Light of the Creator, there is a process that I have to go through." Our logic wants to dictate or make sense of process, but this kabbalistic teaching and these verses give us the strength to actualize assistance and elevation from the Creator in an instant, in a blink of an eye.

MAINTAINING RELATIONSHIPS
WITH APPRECIATION

The Bible says that Joseph's brothers came down to Egypt, and after a time, Joseph asked them to bring their brother Benjamin to him. It is important to mention that after the loss of Joseph, Jacob loved Benjamin the most of all the brothers and held him dear. Benjamin was brought to Egypt to meet Joseph, but like the other brothers, Benjamin did not recognize Joseph. Joseph gave the brothers the grain that they had come to Egypt to collect, but as the brothers prepared to leave, Joseph told his assistant to hide a silver goblet in Benjamin's bag. Then after the brothers had departed, Joseph sent his soldiers to arrest them for stealing the goblet.

The brothers, with Benjamin, were dragged back to Egypt. Joseph told the brothers that Benjamin would have to remain a slave in Egypt as a consequence of his stealing. The brothers, in anguish, thought that not only had they lost their brother Joseph, but now their brother Benjamin would be lost to them as well. What was Joseph's reason for creating this entire drama, that necessitated the separation of Benjamin from his brothers? Why did Joseph choose this particular pretext as a way of ultimately revealing his true identity to his brothers?

The kabbalists tell us that these twelve children of Jacob were not simply people. They were great chariots of Light, great channels of the Light of the Creator. Each of them had his own spiritual task, his own spiritual channel, his own spiritual job. The job of Joseph was to gather all of the Lights before they could be revealed in our world. Joseph contained the power that would unite all the disparate Lights and prepare them for manifestation.

When Joseph was sold down into Egypt, all the brothers began to falter spiritually. They did not know why, thinking that the timing was just a coincidence. Yehuda began falling spiritually, and so did the rest of the brothers because they had pushed their brother Joseph aside, and Joseph was the force that held them together and elevated them. Often when we are not aware of those people in our life who sustain us both physically and spiritually, we do not appreciate their assistance and the need that we have for them. It is only when those people are either taken away or step out of our life that we begin to realize how much we needed them.

The kabbalists teach that when Joseph was separated from his brothers, Benjamin took his place spiritually. Although Benjamin was not on the level of Joseph, he still began bringing unity and spiritual elevation to the rest of his brothers. Although the brothers had begun a new level of elevation with the spiritual assistance of Benjamin, they did not attribute this growth to him. They honestly did not know the reason why they were able to begin elevating spiritually once more. Joseph knew, however, and he realized that the only way to awaken their appreciation for the assistance that Benjamin was giving them was to separate him from his brothers. This was the reason why the silver goblet was put in Benjamin's bag.

This separation from Benjamin was the first time the brothers began to truly appreciate the assistance Benjamin was giving to them, and it allowed them to begin the process of reunifying with both Benjamin and with their long-lost brother, Joseph. Joseph understood that if his brothers did not begin an awakening of appreciation for the spiritual support their brother, Benjamin, was bringing to them, they would not achieve their ultimate potential, their goal in life. And certainly they would not achieve the ultimate level of unity that was essential between these great spiritual giants. Through their renewed appreciation for Benjamin, they also awakened a greater appreciation for the loss of Joseph, thereby earning the merit to be reunified with both Benjamin and Joseph.

There are some lessons in this story that contain at their core a very important message. Each one of us has in our life those people whom we appreciate, but the truth is that there are other people who assist us in physical and spiritual ways for whom we do not have enough appreciation, or even no appreciation at all. The sad reality is that if we do not awaken an appreciation for these people in our lives, these relationships will falter, leading to separation. The only thing we can do to ensure that we do not lose the Benjamins and Josephs in our lives—those people whom we have not appreciated for their spiritual assistance—is to proactively awaken an appreciation for their support, for their Light.

We have to be aware and perhaps even slightly afraid that if we do not awaken within ourselves a strong enough true appreciation for these people, separation (lasting or momentary) will be the result. Only once we have a true and growing appreciation for these people who are giving us assistance in our lives can we truly receive from them all of the Light that they can give us, all of the support that they can give us.

So a very important lesson from Joseph and his brothers, then, is the realization that there are people in our lives who are supporting us but whom we might not even be aware of, whom we certainly do not appreciate or appreciate enough. And if we want to ensure that their support remains with us, we have to be constantly awakening ourselves to have a greater and greater appreciation for what they give us. Only if we are constantly growing in that appreciation can we be guaranteed to keep that support and our relationship.

TRUE FRIENDSHIP AND LOVE

The third idea that that I would like to share takes us back to Joseph and Pharaoh's head wine steward. The Bible says that when Joseph was in jail, he interpreted dreams. Joseph interpreted the dream of Pharaoh's wine steward, who was in jail with him at the time. Joseph informed the wine steward that his dream meant that he would soon be released from the jail, elevated to his previous post, and once again be at Pharaoh's side, pouring wine for him.

The Bible says that Joseph asked the wine steward, "When you are released from jail, please remember me." The kabbalists ask, "Why did Joseph try to ingratiate himself with this other prisoner and ensure that the wine steward remembered him? Did Joseph not trust that the Light of the Creator would come and assist him to elevate out of his darkness?" Joseph spent two additional years in prison as a consequence of his request to the wine steward, specifically because of his lack of certainty in the Light of the Creator. So what was it about this relationship with the wine steward that was so important to Joseph?

A great kabbalist, the Arvei Nachal reveals to us in his work a tremendous secret that not only explains this relationship but also gives us a very important life-lesson. He says that when two people achieve a level of bond, of friendship, of love, so complete that each puts the well-being of the other above his own, wanting good not for him- or herself but for the other person, then the Creator will set aside all His other concerns in order to draw down Light upon these two people. As we act in this world, so we awaken acts from Above.

When the love between two people is so true and complete that each desires goodness for his or her friend before themselves, this awakens a tremendous flow of Light from Above. The kabbalists explain that the Creator, no matter what else He is dealing with, focuses completely on bringing Light and blessings to these two people. Conversely, if two people do not have this perfect selfless love—even if there is no hatred between them—they cannot receive this tremendous flow of blessings from Above.

The Arvei Nachal says that whenever we find ourselves in need of tremendous Light from Above, we should use this teaching. We should find a friend whom we can truly bond with in this way, and through an awakening of this kind of friendship, draw a tremendous amount of Light into our life. This is a very practical understanding. The kabbalists explain, however, that most of us do not have this type of friendship. Although we have close friends whom we care about, it is very unusual to find someone whose ultimate desire is to take care of his friend's needs before his own.

So when we find ourselves in a difficult situation, the Arvei Nachal teaches us that one of the great spiritual tools that we can use is to find a friend in whom we truly can invest ourselves completely. If we do—and if that friend reciprocates with an equally selfless love—the Creator will set aside everything else to come and assist us, even if previously we did not merit this assistance. Finding one person for whom we can love so completely and so wholly that that person's desires come before our own enables us to awaken a much greater and more direct source of blessings and fulfillment in our own life.

The Arvei Nachal relates this teaching to the story of Joseph and the wine steward. Joseph found himself in jail for ten years.

He had suffered tremendous hardship and had tried all the spiritual tools he knew, but nothing had helped him. Then Joseph remembered this one last tool. If he could find someone for whom he could awaken true love, a friend whose needs he could place above his own, then he could draw to himself the assistance from Above to be released from jail.

So when the wine steward came to Joseph to have his dream interpreted, Joseph realized that this man was also in a place of lack and he thought, "Maybe I can awaken a tremendous friendship with this person and our love will be so perfect, so strong, that it will be able to bring assistance from Above for both of us." Unfortunately, although Joseph tried to awaken true love between them, we learn that Joseph's love for the wine steward was not reciprocated. Joseph remained in jail for two more years because the wine steward did not reach the point where Joseph's desires and needs came before his own, a prerequisite for the assistance from Above. Both parties in the relationship must feel truly selfless love to draw down tremendous Light.

Although finding real love did not work out for Joseph while he was in jail, we can still take this teaching and apply it in our own life. Although Joseph tried to use this tool when he was in difficulty, clearly we can use it at any point in our life—the amount of blessings and assistance is limitless.

Rav Brandwein shared with my father, the Rav, a story that I think truly illustrates this point. It is always special for me to be able to share teachings that I heard from my father who heard them from his teacher.

Story: "Please Let Me Die for You"

Hundreds of years ago, there was a man who did something for which the king condemned him to death. After hearing the sentence, the man turned to the king and asked, "Could I please have a week to put my affairs in order?"

The king replied, "I would like grant you this wish, but I am concerned that you will not return to face your sentence, that you will run away. If you can find somebody who will stay in your place while I set you free for a week to put your affairs in order, I will let you go. But bear in mind, if you are not back in time to face your sentence—even if you are only a minute late—I will kill your friend instead. However, if you do come back before one week is up, the sentence will be carried out on you as was intended."

This man went to his very closest friend, whom he had loved since childhood, and asked him, "Can you please do me this favor? I need a week to put my affairs in order before the king has me executed. I need you to replace me in the jail for one week so that the king will allow me to go."

His friend replied, "Of course, I will go to jail in your place; I would do anything for you."

The week went by, and the man put his affairs in order. But then he ran into delays on the road back and was a little late in returning to the jail. The king decided, "This man has not kept his promise, so I have no choice but to carry out his death sentence on his friend." The guards escorted the friend to the gallows to prepare for his hanging.

Just then the man originally sentenced to death ran toward the gallows, yelling, "I'm here! I'm here! I was just a little late, but I'm here! I am the one who was sentenced to death, so I am the one who must die. Set my friend free and put me in his place."

But the friend started yelling back, "No, the seven days have passed! According to the terms of your agreement, my friend can no longer be put to death. Now I am the one who is supposed to be put to death!" And they both started pleading their cases before the king, each begging that he should be the one put to death instead of his friend.

The king, seeing the selfless love between these two friends, called for silence. "My decree called for the death of one person, but I see that the bond between you is so complete that if I carry out the sentence, I will be killing two people. Thus I am forced to annul my original decree. You may both go free."

Rav Brandwein taught my father, the Rav, many lessons from this story, but one lesson that I want to share is that if we can awaken one true love in our life, one true mutual friendship that is based on placing our friend's needs before our own, not only will we remove a tremendous amount of judgment from our lives, but this true and pure friendship will allow a tremendous flow of Light and blessings to come to us. May we all merit in our lives one such true friendship!

Vayigash

HOLY AUDACITY

The story of Vayigash begins with the words: *"Vayigash elav Yehuda"* (Yehuda stood up to Joseph). It is no coincidence that Vayigash is generally read on the Shabbat after *Chanukah* because there is a similarity of consciousness between the Maccabees (*Hashmonaim*) who defeated the Greeks and the story of Vayigash.

What the kabbalists explain, and the *Zohar* makes clear, is we are not simply discussing a story that happened thousands of years ago; this is our actual process of the Redemption. The Final Redemption can only come when enough people take upon themselves the mantle, the ability to "rise up," just as Yehuda rose up to Joseph and the Maccabees rose up against Antiochus.

Vayigash elav Yehuda is our elevation with what the sages call *azut dekedusha* (holy audacity). Rising up with holy audacity is what achieved the miracle of Chanukah. The reason a few Maccabees were able to defeat the powerful Greek army was not because they had phenomenal physical strength or capability; the miracle was made possible because they had *azut dekedusha*, and *vayigash elav Yehuda*. They stood up against the Greeks with holy audacity.

In the previous story of Miketz, Yehuda and his brothers were beaten down by Joseph and the challenging events presented to them. This is, unfortunately, where we and the world are today—we are still beaten down by the *Galut*, by the darkness in our world.

Vayigash changes all that. Yehuda said, "Even if we do not deserve to, even if it is not necessarily correct, we are going to stand up." The great gift of the Shabbat of Vayigash is that it awakens from within the strength to stand up.

I have a student who owns a business that helps many clients and large companies. This particular student is very down-to-earth and so are his clients. I asked him what was so unique about his service. He replied, "If you want to know what it is that my clients receive from me, it is nothing more than the strength to act on their own convictions." Giving someone the strength to act on his or her convictions struck me as a very enlightening concept.

Spiritual strength is one of the elements most missing in our world today. The reason the miracle of *Chanukah* occurred was not because of anyone's merit or their spiritual level; it was because the *Hashmonaim* achieved *azut dekedusha*, this spiritual strength. We are meant to raise our hearts in our spiritual work, and this is the overarching gift of the Shabbat of Vayigash.

NAKDIMON BEN GURYON'S MIRACLES

In the *Talmud* in *Ta'anit 19b*, there is a story of Nakdimon ben Guryon.

We know that during the *Shlosha Regalim* (the holidays of *Pesach, Shavuot,* and *Sukkot*), many Israelites as well as international visitors come to Jerusalem to celebrate these cosmic events. During one such time, many more people than expected came to the city, and there was no water for them to drink.

Nakdimon ben Guryon, a very remarkable and wealthy man, lived in Jerusalem at that time. In fact there is discussion among scholars as to whether this Nakdimon is the same Nakdimon mentioned in the New Testament. But in either case, he was a very noteworthy character.

Nakdimon went to another wealthy man who owned wells of water and asked, "Let me borrow twelve wells of water from you so all the people who are in Jerusalem can drink. I promise that by a specified date, I will make sure to pay you back with twelve wells filled with water. And if on that day I am not able to give you those twelve wells of water, I promise to give you twelve pieces of silver." In those days, twelve pieces of silver was an enormous amount of money.

The wealthy man and Nakdimon agreed on a specific date for the payback. It did not rain all year, though, and when it came time for Nakdimon to pay the wealthy man back with twelve holes filled with water, he could not. Nakdimon had assumed that it would rain and that the twelve holes that he had dug would be filled with water in time to repay the wealthy man.

On the morning of the day he was to repay the wealthy man, the wealthy man sent Nakdimon a message: "Give me the water if you have it, or give me the money. Today is the day you agreed to pay me back." Nakdimon sent a message back to the wealthy man: "Do not worry, I have all day to pay you back." That afternoon, Nakdimon received another message: "Pay me back the water or money," to which Nakdimon replied: "There is still some time left in the day." Toward sunset, a third message arrived: "Give me the water or the money." Again Nakdimon replied: "Do not worry, I still have time in the day to repay you."

The wealthy man laughed when he heard this reply. It had not rained all year. Did Nakdimon really think that in the next few hours of this day, enough rain was going to fall to fill up his twelve wells with water? While he waited, the wealthy man went to the bathhouse.

At the same time, Nakdimon decided to go the temple, because he was anxious and did not want to pay so much money to the wealthy man. He covered his head with his *Talit* (prayer shawl) and began to pray. He said to the Creator, "Master of the world, You know why I borrowed these twelve wells of water. It was not for me. It was not for my family. I did it for You."

The moment Nakdimon finished his prayer, the rain fell with tremendous force and filled to overflowing the twelve wells with water.

The wealthy man exited the bathhouse at the same time Nakdimon left the temple. They met in the street and Nakdimon jokingly said to the wealthy man, "Now you owe me some money because these wells of repayment are overflowing with water. I am giving you back more than I borrowed."
The wealthy man answered, "I know that the only reason it rained today is because of you. The Creator changed the world for you. But if I wanted to, I could still complain. I could say that now that it is dark because it is overcast, it rained after the sun had already set. Therefore, it really rained on my day, not yours, and you still have to pay me the money."

So Nakdimon went back into the temple, covered himself with his *Talit* once more, and prayed. Nakdimon said to the Creator, "Master of the world, let the world know that You have beloved people in this world and that I am truly connected to You." Immediately, the clouds disappeared, the sky cleared, and the sun began to shine.

The wealthy man said to Nakdimon, "You know, even if the sun did not shine now, I could still continue arguing with you."

Here we have a story that contains two miracles. First, Nakdimon said to the Creator, "The only reason that I now owe this man the water is because I did it for You," and the Creator immediately created the miracle of rain. It had not rained for an entire year, but when Nakdimon truly asked for it, the rain came. The second miracle occurred when Nakdimon went back into the temple and prayed again to the Creator, "Let the world know that I am truly connected to You," and the sun shone. I think the second miracle is the greater of the two because with the first miracle, Nakdimon was desperate: It had not rained all year, and he did not want to repay the wealthy man with money. It was a great miracle, but it was a miracle born of desperation.

The second miracle occurred when Nakdimon awakened his *azut dekedusha* and said, "No, I control this world." Nakdimon could have argued with the wealthy man for many hours and probably could have won, but instead, he went back into the temple and prayed, "Let them know that I am connected to You." Thus, the second miracle is more significant than the first miracle.

Many people, when they are desperate, ask the Creator to come and assist them, but not enough of us have the holy audacity to say, "We are going to make the world change. We are going to tell the Creator that He has to create this miracle." *Azut dekedusha* is what is missing in our world—

and what is missing from us. It is what is missing for the *Gemar HaTikkun* (Final Redemption) to come. It is what is missing for *Mashiach* consciousness and for *bila hamavet lanetzach* (immortality) to come to this world. The lesson for us is to not just find the strength for ourselves, but also to give this strength to the world.

The *Talmud* explains that every person has to say, "This entire world was created for me," meaning that even if there is nothing else in this world, I am here and everything was created for me. But this consciousness of "everything was created for me" comes with responsibility. Obviously, if we are just wasting our lives, if we are not fulfilling our potential and doing what we are meant to do, then we cannot say, "Everything was created for me." But if we are truly trying to manifest our potential in this world, to accomplish what we came to this world to achieve, then we need to say, "This entire creation was created for me." This is a very important consciousness that we have to awaken within ourselves.

Vayigash elav Yehuda is what Yehuda awakens within us on the Shabbat of Yayigash. The *Zohar* says that *vayigash elav Yehuda* is not about Yehuda standing up to Joseph; its meaning is much more profound than that. *Vayigash elav Yehuda* is about the Israelites coming to the Creator and saying, "We are going to argue with You, the Creator. We are going to say things You might not want to hear. We are going to have a little bit of *chutzpah*, and we are going to stand up."

Mashiach cannot come and the *Gemar HaTikkun* cannot be achieved until we attain this level of holy audacity. This holy audacity, however, has to be coupled with the life that we lead. We cannot come to the Creator with nothing and have holy audacity. Yet we do not have to be perfect either. Yehuda was not perfect, the *Hashmonaim* were not perfect, nor was Nakdimon ben Guryon, but they all had holy audacity.

HE ELEVATES HIMSELF AND ELEVATES HIS GENERATION

There is a beautiful section in the *Midrash* that says that when the Creator created our world, He saw the end—meaning, He created the potential for the great Light that will be revealed in our world, the great Light that will end the darkness of this world. It is the Light that will be revealed in our world through what we call *Mashiach,* or "end of the correction." It is the moment when humanity, as a critical mass, has completed the work to remove the darkness and pain from our world.

At The Kabbalah Centre, we teach about *bila hamavet lanetzach*—immortality—the removal of pain and suffering from our world forever. For many of us, this is a difficult concept to truly internalize. Do you know who else has trouble accepting this concept? In the *Midrash,* it says that the most negative of angels, the Satan, also did not believe that immortality was possible. The Satan said to the Creator,

"Master of the World, this great Light that is hidden with You, God, who is it for?" The Creator answered, "This great Light is prepared for those who are going to embarrass you, who are going to finish you off." The Satan was surprised at this answer. He thought he would go on forever; that his job of inflicting pain, suffering, and death would last for all time.

Satan was surprised by the revelation that there would come a time when this Light, prepared and held by the Creator, would bring an end to the darkness. Yet he still did not believe the Creator, so he said, "Show me who this is going to be." The Creator said, "Come and see him." When the Satan, the Angel of Death, saw this great Light, he fell on his face. Completely shaken up, he said, "This is the strength, the Light, that is going to make me fall." The *Midrash* says that here, for the first time, the Satan, the Angel of Death, came to the realization that immortality was inevitable, as he confirmed, "There will come a time when death and suffering will be removed from the world." Then the Satan asked, "How will this Light will be revealed?" The Creator replied—and this is the most important sentence in this *Midrash* and is the key—"He will elevate himself, and he will elevate his generation." My father, the Rav, always says that *Mashiach* is not a person; it is a consciousness. In essence, what the Creator told the Satan, the Angel of Death, is that the singular key, the most important work, the most important consciousness that we have to awaken if we want to bring about the removal of pain and suffering from our lives is this elevation. It is this *azut dekedusha*, holy audacity.

If we continue in our spiritual work and in our connection but do not push ourselves further to achieve this audacity, this *azut*, we cannot reveal this Light and we cannot bring an end to pain, suffering, and darkness in our lives and in the world. The Creator gave away the secret and hopefully awakened it within us. The only way that pain, suffering, and darkness can be removed from our world is if we awaken this audacity within ourselves and come to the realization that there is so much— even beyond our ability and capability—that we can do.

There are so many concepts, so many important understandings to gain in our spiritual journey, but here the Creator tells us the secret, the basis for us to bring about an end to the pain, suffering, and darkness in our lives and in the world. It is the concept of *azut kedusha*, holy audacity that we must awaken, not because we are so spiritually elevated but because we want to awaken it for the sake of sharing.

The miracle that Nakdimon ben Guryon was able to awaken was not because of his spiritual elevation. Yehuda, in Vayigash, was able to bring an end to the pain of his entire family, not because of his spiritual elevation but because he awakened this desire of holy audacity within himself. One of the greatest gifts of the Shabbat of Vayigash is that Yehuda comes back and gives those of us who desire this strength, the ability to awaken this *azut*, this audacity within ourselves. We have to desire this audacity; we have to understand that everything that we have done until now—all the work, all of our connections—can bring us up to the wall.

But the wall remains. How do we break through the wall that still keeps us in darkness, that still keeps pain in our lives, that still keeps darkness and pain in our world? We can break through with the audacity to say, "I am going to ask for and receive beyond my capabilities." Nakdimon did it. Yehuda did it on the Shabbat of Vayigash. We all have the ability and capability to bring an end to pain, suffering, and darkness in our lives and in the world, but only, as the *Midrash* says, when we "raise ourselves up"—raising not our capability but the strength to ask beyond what we can do. Every one of us must ask for this assistance, not because we deserve it, not because we spiritually earned it, but because we want to create a change in our world, we want to create a change in our lives.

The secret of "He will elevate himself, and he will elevate his generation"—*Mashiach*—is what the Creator revealed to the Angel of Death. This secret consciousness is what will bring an end to the darkness of our world. All the spiritual work that we do can bring Light into our lives and Light into this world, but if we want to create a true change, we have to ask for *azut dekedusha—chutzpah*, audacity. We have to be able to say to the Creator, "No, the first miracle You did for me is not enough. I'm doing this not for myself, I am doing this for others. I am doing this for the world." And because we ask for more, because we ask for greater assistance, for more miracles, more Light, we are not simply drawing upon our own strength. We are not asking for what we deserve; we are not asking for our capabilities. We are asking for something beyond all that!

Story: "Make Sure to Tell Them That I Was Here Before..."

Recently, on a flight back from Miami, my son David, read me a story that goes back a few hundred years.

One day, Rabbi Aharon of Karlin got a message that he needed to go to a particular village, situated in the middle of nowhere, and pray there. So he gathered a few of his students, and they traveled by carriage to the village. The journey was long and it was almost night when they finally arrived at the village. Rabbi Aharon disembarked from the carriage and walked with his students to a house. They knocked on the door and a very old man opened it. The old man smiled when he saw who it was and said, "I have been waiting for you. Please come in."

Rabbi Aharon and his students entered the house, and because of the late hour, they began the evening prayers. While they were praying, Rabbi Aharon suddenly realized that this old man had been truly waiting for them, and he understood that they needed to reveal a tremendous amount of Light in this town. So he prayed with more vigor and his students joined him, yelling and singing and dancing. None of them noticed the time go by.

They made so much noise that they woke up the entire village, who thought the ruckus meant that there was a fire somewhere. In those days, there were no fire stations, so if there was a fire in the village, everyone would get together, go to the well, get water, and help to put out the fire. So the entire village got up out of their beds, dashed to the well, and then ran toward this old man's house with their buckets of water. When the villagers got to the house, they found all the windows open, and saw that not only was there no fire, but people were dancing and singing inside. Captivated by the singing and dancing and the energy of Rabbi Aharon and his students, the villagers quickly joined in the festivities.

The happy festivities progressed into a feast of food and drink. There was so much joy and so much Light that the students of Rabbi Aharon commented that it had the taste of *Mashiach* (Messiah), the taste of the Final Redemption.

When Rabbi Aharon of Karlin and his students were preparing to leave the village, they went to the old man to say goodbye. The old man stopped them and said, "I want you to know that today is my one hundred and seventh birthday. A hundred years ago when my father owned this very inn, the Baal Shem Tov with his students came to spend the night. They did exactly what you and your students did here last night. They prayed. They yelled, and sang, and danced, and the whole town joined in with them. When the Baal Shem Tov was about to leave, he turned to me, gave me a blessing, and said, 'Young boy, one hundred years from now, another great spiritual master will come here with his students, and they are going to do the same thing we have done. Make sure you tell them that I was here, and that we did this first.'"

This story teaches us that everything we do—whether truly awakening within ourselves the *azut dekedusha* (holy audacity) to create miracles, or striving for the ability to "stand up" and create change—has been achieved by someone before us. Yehuda was here first and he did it for us. The *Hashmonaim* were here first and they did it for us. Nakdimon ben Guryon was here first and he did it for us. We are not creating new pathways, nor are we awakening anything new. We are simply reigniting and reconnecting to the pathways to the miracles that all the great spiritual giants have laid for us throughout history.

The *Tana Devei Eliyahu* says that we have to constantly ask ourselves: "When will my actions achieve the level of the great actions of Abraham, Isaac, and Jacob?" What does this mean? It does not mean that our spiritual work will be as great as Abraham, Isaac, and Jacob's, but that when we awaken our holy audacity, our actions will awaken the actions of these spiritual giants.

We know we cannot create miracles, or bring Messiah or the Final Redemption on our own, but those spiritual giants who were here first have paved the way for us. This is what Yehuda does on the Shabbat of Vayigash. Yehuda comes back each year and gives us this holy audacity.

How do we merit receiving this strength? We merit the holy audacity by reminding ourselves that our actions reawaken what those before us accomplished and that we are only reconnecting to what they did. We can create miracles because they opened up this channel for us.

In the *Hallel* prayer, we say, *"Pitchu li sharei tzedek avobam odecha,"* a verse that King David wrote. We ask the Creator, "Open for me the gates," without saying the word "please." This is the level we have to achieve, where we can come to the Creator and say, "Open for me the gates," and then *"Odecha"* (I will thank You).

Nakdimon said, "This is not for me, not for my family, but because I want to do Your work." When we come to the Creator with this consciousness and say, "You have to give me this strength, You have to give me this power, You have to create this miracle because I want to do it to reveal Light in this world," this throws open all the Gates of Light to flood into our world. This gift of Vayigash is tremendously powerful and completely necessary—because without this gift, *Mashiach* cannot come.

Vayechi

JACOB TOOK UPON HIMSELF
THE CORRECTION AND PAIN OF ADAM

The Baal Shem Tov tells us that it is not a coincidence when different topics we study relate to each other; it is a sign from the Creator.

The Torah (Bible) says that Jacob lived in Egypt for seventeen years. The *Zohar* explains that the Torah does not say that Jacob was in Egypt for seventeen years; it says he *lived* in Egypt for seventeen years, implying that before this point, Jacob's life was not truly being lived. According to the Torah, it was only in his last seventeen years that Jacob lived.

The *Zohar* asks why Jacob was not truly alive during most of his life. Before entering Egypt, Jacob's life was filled with pain and sadness. It was only once Jacob went to Egypt that we say "he lived." When Jacob arrived in Egypt, he saw that his son

Joseph was second-in-command to Pharaoh. Jacob saw his children and grandchildren—all seventy members of his family—in Egypt.

While Jacob lived in the land of Israel, he had no joy. It was only once Jacob went down into Egypt (the source of all the exiles) that he actually lived. We learn from Jacob's life that if a person is truly connected to the Light of the Creator, it is in the greatest darkness that he or she can have the greatest Light.

The *Zohar* says the first word of this story— *"Vayechi"* (And he lived)—indicates that Jacob only experienced joy in the last seventeen years of his life. The Shem Mishmuel (Rabbi Shmuel Bornsztain, 1856–1926) says, "We can understand that the life of people on a lower spiritual level is not considered 'life' because of their pain and hardship. But how can we identify this concept with Jacob? Jacob lived his life connected to the Light of the Creator, so how can we say that for the first years of his life he was in pain? How can we say that all those first years of his life are not considered 'life?'"

Rabbi Isaac Luria (the Ari) says in *Likutei Torah* that the first hundred and thirty years Jacob lived in Israel were the years that Jacob was correcting the sin of Adam. This correction concerned the *Brit* (Covenant) between God and man. One of the physical manifestations of damage to the Covenant— damage to the sexual aspect of one's being—is that it brings heaviness and sadness and lack of what we call *chiut* (excitement, life) to the person who has done the damage.

When a person has purified himself of the damage he has caused to the Brit, then he has true life and true joy.

The Ari says that the amount of joy we have in our life is a great indication of whether we have corrected this damage or not. If we feel joy and excitement in our spiritual work, if we feel joy and excitement in our prayers, and on Shabbat, and in our connection to the *Zohar*, then we know that we have corrected this damage. To the degree that one lacks excitement and joy in a spiritual connection, he or she has not corrected this damage.

Although Jacob was purer than almost anyone who had ever lived, he took it upon himself to correct the hundred and thirty years of damage of Adam, and therefore, he had to take on the manifestation of this damage as well. Every morning that Jacob woke up, he had a choice to make: "Jacob you are perfect, almost more perfect than Abraham and Isaac, more perfect than anybody who's ever lived. Do you want to manifest this? Do you want to just have an amazing day today? Or do you want to continue this unbelievably tough work of the correction of Adam, which is going to result in a day heavy with sadness? This is your choice, Jacob. What are you going to do?"

And every morning for those hundred and thirty years, Jacob arose to face this choice, and he chose pain: He chose to continue the correction of Adam. He took upon himself the *ibur* (soul) and damage of Adam so that he could correct it. What an amazing revelation this is.

As long as Jacob had not completed this correction, he knew it meant that he could not experience the joy that was destined to be his. This is why the *Zohar* says that during those first hundred and thirty years, Jacob did not have life. Only when he went down into Egypt, after he had finished the correction of Adam, did Jacob have life. That is why the Torah says that when Jacob lived in Egypt, "he had life."

Can you imagine what it must have been like for Jacob, knowing that everything he had experienced until the time of entering Egypt was not his? None of the pain, none of the darkness, none of the correction was for himself. For the first hundred and thirty years of Jacob's life, whom was he living for? Whom was he correcting for? Who was he in pain for? Jacob was in pain because of Adam. He was in pain for us.

Once Jacob had finished the correction, the Creator said, "That is it, Jacob, you have done it. There is no more pain that you need to take upon yourself." Now Jacob could live the next seventeen years for himself. We have to understand that all of the difficulties in Jacob's life—Esau wanting to kill him, Laban cheating him, Joseph being sold as slave and Jacob being separated from him all those years—didn't happen because of Jacob. These events occurred because Jacob woke up each morning and he took upon himself the pain of Adam. What an awesome understanding.

There is Always an Opening for Doubt

The *Zohar* asks: "Why could Jacob not see that Joseph was alive? After all, Jacob had *Ruach HaKodesh* (Divine Inspiration)." To which the *Zohar* answers: "Because the *Shechinah* could not rest upon Jacob all those years he was in pain." All the years that Joseph was away from him, Jacob did not have complete Divine Inspiration, and therefore was not able to see that Joseph was alive. It was not simply that Jacob was sad because Joseph was not there with him, he was sad because every morning he decided to take upon himself more of the correction of Adam. It is easy to see how there was a powerful opening for doubt to enter Jacob's life.

Most of us, when we take upon ourselves important work, would still question, "I have to run away from my brother? I have to fight with my father-in-law? I have to lose my most beloved son?"

Jacob did not know that these traumatic events were connected to the *tikkun* (correction) of Adam that he took upon himself. The Creator did not come and say to him, "Look, today you are going to lose your son because of the work that you took upon yourself." This was never made clear to Jacob. This lack of clarity was also part of the correction. So Jacob woke up each morning and said, "I am willing to continue in this pain." Jacob did not know that taking on this pain meant that he was going to lose his beloved son to slavery, or that his father-in-law, Laban, was going to cheat him out of everything. So the opening for doubt was enormous.

Never in the history of humanity has one person corrected so much. Jacob woke up every day for a hundred and thirty years and said, "I am willing to take this difficult work upon myself." Jacob never questioned how such tragedy could befall him. He never asked the Creator, "How could You take my son away from me? How could You make all this trouble with my brother? How could You make all this trouble with my father-in-law?

We know in retrospect that the reason why all these things happened to Jacob was because of Adam's correction that he took upon himself, but the Creator never told him this. Can you imagine how much easier it would have been if the Creator had at least helped Jacob make this association?

One of the great lessons we learn from Jacob is that there has to always be an opening for doubt for us to complete our correction. Therefore, he was never told that the reason why his life looked that way was because of the work that he took upon himself.

The *Galut* (Exile) and the pain and suffering we experience today are probably not even a tenth of one percent of what they could have been, had Jacob not made Adam's correction. For one hundred and thirty years, tremendous pain and darkness was foisted on Jacob so that he could accomplish this correction.

We look at ourselves and sometimes, in our ignorance, we do not understand why certain things occur. "I'm doing so much good work. How could this happen?" We need to understand that what we do, the actions we carry out, do not come close to the spiritual achievements of Jacob, and that whatever our pain is, it is nowhere near the enormous amount of pain that Jacob experienced.

Rabbi Yitzchak Isaac of Komarna wrote that if we experience doubts, we should know that a judgment is, God forbid, meant to come down upon us or our family. This judgment manifests itself in the form of doubt. If we fight off the doubts, we then remove the judgment. Conversely, if we allow the doubts to enter, then, God forbid, we allow the impending judgment to manifest. This is a very important teaching! When we fight off our doubts, we avert the judgment that was meant for us, but if we succumb to our doubts, then we allow that judgment to, God forbid, manifest in our lives.

How Much Pain Am I Willing to Accept to Help Another Person?

Just imagine being able to carry out a tremendously difficult task while experiencing incredible pain, while never allowing yourself to succumb to any doubt. One of the gifts Jacob gives us on the Shabbat of Vayechi is the ability to awaken ourselves to the realization that we are nowhere near his level. Part of our spiritual work needs to involve taking upon ourselves the pain of others. We should ask ourselves, "How much pain am I willing to take upon myself to help another person?" To the degree that we are willing to take upon ourselves the pain of another person, we help them with their correction—and achieve our own.

When we sit comfortably giving advice and assistance to others, we may achieve something, but we cannot truly correct ourselves or help others to correct themselves unless we are willing to take upon ourselves some degree of their pain. To sit and meditate on another person's pain and internalize it is not what we are speaking about here. With Jacob, the pain came from outside of himself, from his brother wanting to kill him, for instance; it was not related to the *work* that Jacob was doing personally.

When we open up this door, it can be frightening because we do not know where the pain will come from. And yet we still have to be willing to take upon ourselves some degree of this pain in order to assist the correction of others.

BEING JOYOUS ENABLES US TO RECEIVE THE "ADDITIONAL SOUL"

Jacob is called by two names in the Torah: Jacob and Israel. The *Ohr haChaim* (Rabbi Chaim ben Attar, 1696–1743) asked, "Why, when the Torah speaks about the seventeen joyous years of Jacob, does the Torah not refer to Jacob as 'Israel'?" The Torah should say: *Israel* lived in the land of Egypt instead of *Jacob* lived in the land of Egypt. The name "Israel" represents a higher level than Jacob, so why does the Torah say "Jacob" instead?

The name "Israel"—besides all the elevated spiritual levels it represented—was also indicative of Jacob's happy times, when Jacob was joyous. Whenever Jacob was happy, he was called "Israel," and whenever he was sad, he was called "Jacob."

It is important to understand that there are two parts to our soul. Each soul has a "Jacob" and an "Israel." The lower part of our soul—which we live with most of the time—is called Jacob. The higher part of our soul—which is connected to the Light of the Creator—is called Israel. When the Torah mentions Jacob and Israel, the Torah is actually speaking about us—the lower part of our soul that feels sadness and the higher part of our soul that feels joy and is truly connected to the Light of the Creator.

When we say that on Shabbat, we receive the "additional soul," this means that we have an opportunity to draw the pure, higher part of our soul to us. Because the additional soul that comes on Shabbat connects us to the name "Israel," it is important for us to understand that if we are sad on Shabbat, we will push the additional soul—the higher level part of our soul—away. The same was true for Jacob. He could only manifest the higher part of his soul when he was joyous.

The *Zohar* says that at the Binding of Isaac, the angel called to Abraham twice, saying, "Abraham, Abraham." The kabbalists explain that the reason for this repetition was to indicate to us that we have an "Abraham," that part of ourselves (our perfected self) that resides in the Supernal Worlds, plus a second "Abraham," that part of ourselves (our unperfected self) that resides in this world.

One of the great gifts of Shabbat is that when we are joyous, the Supernal, perfected part of ourselves, the additional soul can come into our reality. However, if we are sad or depressed on Shabbat, the additional soul cannot come down into our life.

Story: The Crying of the Souls

We are taught that drinking something warm immediately after Shabbat helps us with our correction. One evening after Shabbat, while a great kabbalist sat in meditation, one of his students brought him something warm to drink. The kabbalist's eyes were closed, and he was obviously deep in thought. After an hour, the drink got cold. So his student brought him another cup filled with something warm to drink. This drink, too, got cold. When the student brought the kabbalist a third cup of something warm to drink, he saw his teacher open his eyes. So the student asked him, "What were you thinking about?"

The teacher answered, "Every Friday night, the perfect part of our soul, comes down into our world and there is a correction—there is Light that this perfect part of our soul hopes and desires that we will reveal and manifest. When Shabbat comes to an end, our usual soul asks the additional soul, that perfected part of ourselves, 'Did I achieve anything; did I correct anything?' and if the answer is yes, both parts of the soul are happy. But if the answer is no, then they both begin crying. So sometimes, when the additional soul leaves after Shabbat, it leaves with tremendous pain because we have not corrected anything for it on Shabbat." The teacher looked at his student and continued, "If you could ever hear the crying of souls, it would be impossible to erase the sound from your mind because it is so terribly painful to hear."

Unfortunately, many of us are so disconnected from both parts of our soul that after Shabbat, we do not hear or feel anything. But the lesson from this story is that every Shabbat, we are given an incredible opportunity to interact with our perfect reality, with the perfected part that each one of us possesses.

The kabbalist continued explaining to his student, "Every Shabbat, through our connection to our *Neshama Yetara*, we are given the ability to make a correction. And if we do not feel or do not awaken this joy and anticipation, God forbid, this perfected part of our soul, the additional soul, leaves. So it is only through joy—on Shabbat and even during the week— that we draw a little part of that perfected part of our soul to us. And throughout the week, if we are sad, we push away those elements of the additional soul, those elements of our perfected soul."

This concept of Jacob and Israel is really about us. We cannot be called "Israel" if we are not connected to the perfected part of our soul. If that part of our soul that is called "Israel" has gone away, we are only called "Jacob." The Ohr haChaim went through the whole Torah and identified all the different places where Jacob is called "Jacob" and where Jacob is called "Israel."

From this research, he concluded that whenever Jacob was called "Israel," it was because he was happy, and whenever Jacob was called "Jacob," it was because he was sad.

The lesson here for us is to understand the importance of joy, certainly on Shabbat but even throughout the week. When we understand this on a deeper level, we know that we cannot make any correction unless we are connected to the perfected part of our soul, meaning that we cannot make any correction while we are sad.

Therefore, another gift that is given to us on this Shabbat is to truly connect to the level of Israel, and to understand that if we want to make any corrections, we need to be truly happy in order to connect to the level of Israel.

The Ohr haChaim says that when Jacob was told that Joseph was alive, the soul of Jacob was so happy at this news that it received its additional soul, and Jacob became Israel. But when we look at the Torah Scroll, we notice that there is no space between the story of Vayechi and the previous story of Vayigash. The *Midrash* explains that the reason there is no space is because this is the beginning of the exile, and there was great sadness. This is why the Torah says: *"Jacob lived in the land of Egypt,"* using the name "Jacob" and not "Israel" at the beginning of this story.

THE END IS REVEALED

This is an unbelievably insightful and powerful Shabbat, for many reasons, but the one idea we all have to keep in mind the entire week leading up to the Shabbat of Vayechi is the passage: "Jacob called his children and said, 'Come, gather around me, I want to tell you what will happen at the End of Days, what is going to occur in the time of *Mashiach*, what is going to occur before the *Gemar haTikkun*.'"

The *Midrash* says: "When Jacob wanted to reveal what will happen at the End of Days, the *Shechinah* left him, and he began to speak about other things." The *Midrash* draws an interesting parallel here: It says that Jacob was like the king's closest confidant who, on his deathbed, gathers his children together and says, "Let me tell you all the king's secrets." Suddenly, the king comes into the room and says, "You cannot do this." And Jacob replied, "Oh, yeah," and then he began speaking about other things.

The kabbalists explain that what actually happened there was that Jacob wanted to reveal the end (and he did reveal what will occur at the time of the Final Redemption; it is concealed within the story of Vayechi). But he knew that he could not do it in a way that was obvious. Therefore, all of Jacob's blessings that we read about in Vayechi have their literal meaning, but the true Light of these words is the revelation of the *Gemar haTikkun*. In the *Zohar*, Rabbi Shimon bar Yochai speaks about the curses that appear in the Torah, explaining that although on the surface they look like curses, in truth their real essence is complete blessings, and this is what occurs on the Shabbat of Vayechi as well.

Because this is the one Shabbat of the year where all of the Light of *Mashiach*, the Light of the *Ketz* (End), the Light of the *Gemar HaTikkun* is revealed, we should have appreciation for the importance of this Shabbat. Every one of us, when we participate by hearing the reading of the Torah, can connect to the *Gemar HaTikkun* to one degree or another on this Shabbat.

Every one of us has the opportunity on this Shabbat to connect to the *Ketz*, to connect to the end of pain, suffering, and death—and to the totality of Light that Jacob revealed on this Shabbat. The Talmud writes, "When a person leaves this world, the first question he is asked is: 'Did you wait for the Redemption? Did you expect the *Gemar HaTikkun* every day?'"

Only if we begin living with the consciousness of "I am waiting for the Redemption every day," can we connect to the revelation of Jacob on the Shabbat of Vayechi. There is no other Shabbat of the year where all the Light of the *Gemar HaTikkun* is revealed, only through Jacob, in the Shabbat of Vayechi.

The way to access this great revelation is by awakening within ourselves the constant expectation of the *Gemar HaTikkun* occurring now. When we have this consciousness, we can all, with God's help, bring a tremendous revelation of the *Ketz*, a tremendous revelation of the End, of the *Gemar haTikkun,* into this world.

MORE BOOKS THAT CAN HELP YOU BRING THE WISDOM OF KABBALAH INTO YOUR LIFE

Secrets of the Zohar: Stories and Meditations to Awaken the Heart
By Michael Berg

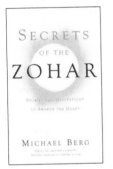

The *Zohar*'s secrets are the secrets of the Bible, passed on as oral tradition and then recorded as a sacred text that remained hidden for thousands of years. They have never been revealed quite as they are here in these pages, which decipher the codes behind the best stories of the ancient sages and offer a special meditation for each one. Entire portions of the *Zohar* are presented, with the Aramaic and its English translation in side-by-side columns. This allows you to scan and to read aloud so that you can draw on the *Zohar*'s full energy and achieve spiritual transformation. Open this book and open your heart to the Light of the *Zohar*!

The Secret History of the Zohar
By Michael Berg

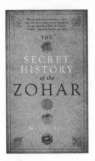

Truth is often stranger than fiction. Many works have been created surrounding the story of the Holy Grail, including, in recent times, the huge bestseller, *The DaVinci Code*. But what if you were to learn that an amazing body of ancient spiritual wisdom and potential source of Light for the world had been "covered up" for centuries and not acknowledged as having had a profound influence on major figures and movements throughout history?

Such is *The Secret History of the Zohar*. It is said that the *Zohar* was hidden in the Ark of the Covenant along with pieces of the first tablets given to Moses. When and how it resurfaced, how it shaped the thinking of the important people who studied it, and how it has survived to flourish in the present day, is the amazing but true story you will find revealed inside this book.

Becoming Like God
By Michael Berg

At the age of 16, kabbalistic scholar Michael Berg began the herculean task of translating The *Zohar*, Kabbalah's chief text, from its original Aramaic into its first complete English translation. The *Zohar*, which consists of 23 volumes, is considered a compendium of virtually all information pertaining to the universe, and its wisdom is only beginning to be verified today.

During the ten years he worked on The *Zohar*, Michael Berg discovered the long-lost secret for which humanity has searched for more than 5,000 years: how to achieve our ultimate destiny. *Becoming Like God* reveals the transformative method by which people can actually break free of what is called "ego nature" to achieve total joy and lasting life.

Berg puts forth the revolutionary idea that for the first time in history, an opportunity is being made available to humankind: an opportunity to Become Like God.

The Secret: Unlocking the Source of Joy & Fulfillment By Michael Berg

The Secret reveals the essence of life in its most concise and powerful form. Several years before the latest "Secret" phenomenon, Michael Berg shared the amazing truths of the world's oldest spiritual wisdom in this book. In it, he has pieced together an ancient puzzle to show that our common understanding of life's purpose is actually backwards, and that anything less than complete joy and fulfillment can be changed by correcting this misperception.

Nano: Technology of Mind over Matter
By Rav Berg

Kabbalah is all about attaining control over the physical world, including our personal lives, at the most fundamental level of reality. It's about achieving and extending mind over matter and developing the ability to create fulfillment, joy, and happiness by controlling everything at the most basic level of existence. In this way, Kabbalah predates and presages the most exciting trend in recent scientific and technological development, the application of nanotechnology to all areas of life in order to create better, stronger, and more efficient results.

The Kabbalah Connection: Preparing the Soul for Pesach
By Rav Berg

Kabbalistically, ego is the source of evil, destruction and suffering in this world. It is the aspect of our nature that separates us from the Light of the Creator, and from our destiny of happiness. *The Kabbalah Connection* describes the powerful spiritual technology built into the system of Creation to help us gain control over the ego. This technology is Passover (*Pesach*).

Each year, the window of time known to many as *Pesach*, gives us the ability to escape this source of misery in our own lives. Although many believe Pesach to be holiday for the Jewish people commemorating their freedom from Egypt, it is in fact, the greatest transformation agent we have against the ego.

Utilizing metaphysics and physics, *The Kabbalah Connection* reveals the consciousness we can utilize the night before *Pesach*, so we can remove the ego and open ourselves up to the Light. This is the necessary step to achieving spiritual fulfillment.

The Kabbalistic Bible
Edited by Yehuda Berg

This five-volume set is a valuable resource for Bible enthusiasts. All five books are edited by, and feature contemporary insights by, noted Kabbalah scholar and teacher, Yehuda Berg. The text is complemented by excerpts from the *Zohar* (the renowned sacred text of Kabbalah), as well as from the writings of four of history's greatest Kabbalists, Rav Isaac Luria (the Ari), Rav Yehuda Ashlag, Rav Yehuda Brandwein, and Rav Berg. Printed front to back, the easy-to-read layout displays Hebrew and English on facing pages, with a simple commentary decoding the mystical secrets of the Torah script on the bottom. The only set available that offers a kabbalistic understanding of the Bible, this special edition boxed set is a perfect gift for the holidays.

Satan: An Autobiography
By Yehuda Berg

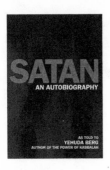

Using the literary device of an "as told to" autobiography, Yehuda Berg explains that Satan is not really the name of a horned devil, but a description of the Adversary that resides within all of us. Manifesting as a recurrent voice of uncertainty and negativity, Satan is actually another name for Ego.

As "Satan" tells us in this book, he is also our "stunt double," whose job it is to take on our pain, if only we would let him. But that requires defeating him in the contests he continually instigates. Now that he is giving away his secrets in this book, we can finally win over the part of ourselves that prevents our connection to the Light, the source of all positive energy.

Simple Light
By Karen Berg

From the woman regarded by many as their "spiritual mother," and whose work has touched millions of lives around the world, here is a book with a message that is simple and straight from the heart: It's all about love and sharing.

Karen's unique voice will serve to inspire you and help you to face life's daily challenges. Open the book to any passage whenever you find a moment, and you will begin to discover the keys to leading a more joyful and fulfilled life.

THE ZOHAR

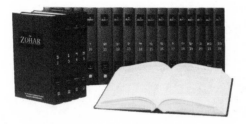

Composed more than 2,000 years ago, the *Zohar* is a set of 23 books, a commentary on biblical and spiritual matters in the form of conversations among spiritual masters. But to describe the *Zohar* only in physical terms is greatly misleading. In truth, the *Zohar* is nothing less than a powerful tool for achieving the most important purposes of our lives. It was given to all humankind by the Creator to bring us protection, to connect us with the Creator's Light, and ultimately to fulfill our birthright of true spiritual transformation.

More than eighty years ago, when The Kabbalah Centre was founded, the *Zohar* had virtually disappeared from the world. Few people in the general population had ever heard of it. Whoever sought to read it—in any country, in any language, at any price— faced a long and futile search.

Today all this has changed. Through the work of The Kabbalah Centre and the editorial efforts of Michael Berg, the *Zohar* is now being brought to the world, not only in the original Aramaic language but also in English. The new English *Zohar* provides everything for connecting to this sacred text on all levels: the original Aramaic text for scanning; an English translation; and clear, concise commentary for study and learning.

THE KABBALAH CENTRE

The Kabbalah Centre is a spiritual organization dedicated to bringing the wisdom of Kabbalah to the world. The Kabbalah Centre itself has existed for more than 80 years, but its spiritual lineage extends back to Rav Isaac Luria in the 16th century and even further back to Rav Shimon bar Yochai, who revealed the principal text of Kabbalah, the *Zohar*, more than 2,000 years ago.

The Kabbalah Centre was founded in 1922 by Rav Yehuda Ashlag, one of the greatest kabbalists of the 20th Century. When Rav Ashlag left this world, leadership of The Kabbalah Centre was taken on by Rav Yehuda Brandwein. Before his passing, Rav Brandwein designated Rav Berg as director of The Kabbalah Centre. Now, for more than 30 years, The Kabbalah Centre has been under the direction of Rav Berg, his wife Karen Berg, and their sons, Yehuda Berg and Michael Berg.

Although there are many scholarly studies of Kabbalah, The Kabbalah Centre does not teach Kabbalah as an academic discipline but as a way of creating a better life. The mission of The Kabbalah Centre is to make the practical tools and spiritual teachings of Kabbalah available to everyone.

The Kabbalah Centre makes no promises. But if people are willing to work hard to grow and become actively sharing, caring and tolerant human beings, Kabbalah teaches that they will then experience fulfillment and joy in a way previously unknown to them.

This sense of fulfillment, however, comes gradually and is always the result of the student's spiritual work.

Our ultimate goal is for all humanity to gain the happiness and fulfillment that is our true destiny.

Kabbalah teaches its students to question and test everything they learn. One of the most important teachings of Kabbalah is that there is no coercion in spirituality.

What Does The Kabbalah Centre Offer?

Local Kabbalah Centres around the world offer onsite spiritual services, lectures, classes, study groups, holiday celebrations and services, and a community of teachers and fellow students. To find a Centre near you, go to www.kabbalah.com.

For those of you unable to access a physical Kabbalah Centre due to the constraints of location or time, we have other ways to participate in The Kabbalah Centre community.

At www.kabbalah.com, we feature online blogs, newsletters, weekly wisdom, a store, and much more.

It's a wonderful way to stay tuned in and in touch, and it gives you access to programs that will expand your mind and challenge you to continue your spiritual work.

Student Support

The Kabbalah Centre empowers people to take responsibility for their own lives. It's about the teachings, not the teachers. But on your journey to personal growth, things can be unclear and sometimes rocky, so it is helpful to have a coach or teacher. Simply call 1 800 KABBALAH toll free.

All Student Support instructors have studied Kabbalah under the direct supervision of Kabbalist Rav Berg, widely recognized as the preeminent kabbalist of our time.

We have also created opportunities for you to interact with other Student Support students through study groups, monthly connections, holiday retreats, and other spiritual events held around the country.

KABBALAH UNIVERSITY

FOUNDED UPON THE TEACHINGS OF RAV BERG

Be in the center of Kabbalah activities anytime and anywhere through ukabbalah.com

Kabbalah University (www.ukabbalah.com) is an online resource center and community offering a vault of wisdom spanning 30 years, and rapidly growing. Removing any time-space limitation, this virtual Kabbalah Centre presents the same courses and spiritual connections as the physical centers, with an added benefit of live streaming videos from worldwide travels. As close as a click of your finger, for a low monthly access fee, it's open 24/7.

Stay current with historic lessons from Rav Berg and inspiring talks with Karen. Delve deeper into Michael Berg's teachings, and journey with Yehuda Berg to holy sites. Connect with world-renowned Kabbalah instructors sharing weekly *Zohar* and consciousness classes that awaken insights into essential life matters such as: relationships, health, prosperity, reincarnation, parenting, and astrology. Check out the library, including hundreds of spiritual topics going back more than four decades. A richer world awaits your presence at ukabbalah.com.

Moses teaches us in Ha'azinu verse 46:

"The Torah is our life because without any spiritual teaching life has no point. When we connect to the Torah we discover our destiny and realize that each one of us has a special job, a particular Light that we come to this physical world to reveal. It is then that life begins to have true meaning."

RACHEL

In honor of your Bat Mitzvah we wish for you to find your true meaning in life and to take your spiritual path with the Light of Rabbi Shimon Bar Yochai and the teachings of the Rav and Karen, Yehuda and Michael to guide you throughout your life.

WITH ALL OUR LOVE,
YOUR FAMILY

Robert and Tsipora
David and Esther
Salvit